Raising Cooperative & Self-Confident Children

A STEP-BY-STEP GUIDE FOR CONSCIOUS PARENTING

FRANCINE C. BEAUVOIR, PH.D.

Pasadena Press

Library of Congress Cataloging-in-Publication Data

Beauvoir, Francine C.
        Raising Cooperative & Self-Confident Children: A step-by-step guide for conscious parenting

        ISBN 0-9667298-0-3

        1. Parenting   2. Self help   3. Psychology

TO BRUCE
my husband and best friend,

and

to our children,
Jon, Dominic, Michelle, and Natalie

TABLE OF CONTENTS

ACKNOWLEDGMENTS

This book was a much greater undertaking than I had ever imagined. Many factors converged to make it happen. First, I want to acknowledge and thank all the people who have written not only on parenting but also on human nature and relationships in general. I am especially thankful for the nurturing of my intellectual development by Harville Hendrix and Alice Miller. Both have had a profound influence on my way of thinking and of understanding my role as a relational human being.

I am also grateful to Jacqueline Lenarsky for her faithful typing of the manuscript, her clearly formulated questions and her suggestions for increased clarification and breadth of the book.

A heartfelt thank you goes to my good friend Cathy Hamilton whose artistry enhances this manuscript throughout. The exquisite touch of her illustrations brings the text to life.

Most of all I want to express my deepest gratitude to my husband, Bruce. He has made the project possible. He has given me hours of manuscript typing, editing, technical advice, as well as being a patient and creative emotional resource, encouraging me to continue and not give up on my dream. His willingness to share my vision has provided me with the energy to complete this project.

Last, but not least, I am extremely thankful to my children, Jon, Dominic, Michelle, and Natalie who have brought me to my knees on many occasions and have taught me so much. I hope I never stop learning from them.

INTRODUCTION

Welcome

Welcome to *"Raising Cooperative And Self Confident Children"*, and congratulations! You want to learn all you can about being a good parent. You have a deep commitment to being the best parent you possibly can. Perhaps, despite your genuine search for answers, your openness to learning, your willingness to follow the best advice of psychologists and child development specialists, you find you are exhausted, depleted, and broken-hearted. And your children are far from the dream you wished for when you began this journey of parenting.

The Parenting Journey

Most of us who venture down that long-winding road called parenthood eventually arrive at a place where we clearly see that our children are not responding to us the way we hoped and expected they would. In our quest for answers, we read what child-rearing "experts du jour" suggest and attempt to employ their advice. What often happens is that the moment our kids "press our buttons," we lose it and soon find ourselves falling right back into the same old power struggles, or maybe even worse ones. In the end, we throw the baby out with the bath water, sighing..."I've read it all and tried it all! Nothing works with my kids."

Hope For The Weary Parent

If the rite of parenthood has lost its luster, if your dreams of the perfect little family have been shattered, if you feel you can only swallow your anger and hold back your tears, this book is for you! Perhaps there are only small bumps along your road of parenthood, but you are always looking for new resources. I invite you also to find comfort in this book. For all parents, this book can be used as a source of renewal, courage and affirmation. I invite your comments and insights.

How To Use This Book

This book provides you with a multifaceted step-by-step program for effective parenting. It is a unique blend of lessons, workbook activities, self-facilitated exercises, and group sharing. It is important to move through the entire process and to take advantage of all the elements in order to receive the full benefit of the program. Make sure you write all exercises, rather than just thinking them out in your mind. Something powerful happens when you do the writing. Something powerful also happens when you share your writing with others.

No single aspect of this process will be more crucial to your success than the formation of a "Partners In Parenting Group" (PIP Group). This support group can be made up of two or more trusted friends, relatives, co-workers or neighbors who are willing to make the commitment to working through this book and meeting at least once every other week— every week, if possible— for sharing and support.

Why is a support group so critical toward changing your relationship with your children? Perhaps the following excerpt from an article by Mary Sykes Wylie, Ph.D., senior editor of The Family Therapy Networker ("Swallowed Alive," Sept/Oct, 1994 issue) says it best:

> "...Even for very good parents, the spells of frustration, grief and tedium that have always been occupational hazards of parenthood were once mitigated by the ready availability of that handy, floating day-care center known as the "local neighborhood." What adult, middle-aged or older, does not remember the open-door policy of their friends' parents: the automatic setting of another place at dinner, the sleepovers... the safe house where a child could go when home was not very inviting. There were safe houses for parents, too, particularly moth-

ers, who could complain about their children, praise one another's and thereby come away reassured that they were doing a decent, if not perfect, job.

Now the houses are closed tight, the parents don't know one another. How could they? They spend almost no time in their own neighborhoods. The result is a pervasive loneliness and isolation... Without community, the very qualities that flow from sustained and dependable human connection - familiarity, affection, sympathy, trust, forbearance, mutual help - disappear."

A safe house, that's what most of us are missing. A place where we can bare our souls and share our dilemmas, our shortcomings and our frustrations with parenting, knowing we are not alone on this most significant of all journeys.

THE HEALING POWER OF GROUPS

I believe that it is only through the personal sharing of emotional pain in a supportive, non-judgmental environment that we can make positive, lasting changes in our lives and our relationships. In fact, this is perhaps the single greatest benefit of therapy. With a truly skilled and devoted counselor, many of us experience unconditional acceptance and validation for the first time in our lives. We can do this for each other! We need to do this for each other! If we as parents do not get the nurturing, support and acceptance we need as adults, we will simply be unable to provide it for our children. We will be too depleted because we can only nourish others to the degree that we receive nourishment. I am absolutely convinced the PIP Groups can be a significant source of that nourishment. However, should you not be ready to contact anyone else, don't be discouraged. Keep reading. This book is still for you.

WHAT IS CONSCIOUS PARENTING, AND DOES IT REALLY PRODUCE COOPERATIVE CHILDREN?

Children love to please their parents! Being cooperative is the natural state of being. This may come as a surprise to you. Maybe your children are not very cooperative. You may say, "They don't listen to me!" But children know unconsciously that their very life is dependent on their parents and they want very much to remain alive. It is to their advantage to cooperate because this brings them the possibility of life. If they are not cooperative at present, it is because they are defending themselves against some intrusion on their lives, and at an unconscious level, they have figured out that being uncooperative is now more life sustaining that being cooperative.

How does becoming a "conscious parent" ensure that your children will become cooperative? Because, by becoming conscious, you will break the chain of unconscious parenting that has gone on for thousands of years. For centuries, parents have been owners and masters of their children. Even in modern times, the reason given to children for obeying has been, "Because your father (mother) said so!" This is commonly thought of as sufficient.

If you do not give careful thought to parenting, research shows that you will parent in the same manner as your parents. You will do the same things - use the same methods - transmit the same legacy that you came from. Another common parenting style is reactive parenting. This is where parents are so upset by the way they were parented that they go to the opposite extreme. If their parents were rigid and controlling, they become liberal with no boundaries. If their parents were liberal with no boundaries, they become rigid and controlling. Doing nothing different or doing the opposite are both reactive parenting and therefore unconscious parenting.

To become conscious parents, we need to become aware that children are subjects and not objects, and that we have as much to learn from them as they do from us. Their input is as important as ours.

In this handbook, you will learn the importance of becoming partners with your children, <u>and</u> you will learn how. Your children have been endowed with wonderful wisdom. We need to learn to consult with them as we struggle to learn both how to nurture them and to set limits for them.

In addition, I will inspire you to become partners with other members of your PIP Group. Nature never intended us to raise children alone. An accepting and loving community is an essential ingredient for good parenting.

One of the greatest gifts you can give your children is developing a conscious marriage. Indeed, it is a must to develop a good working relationship with your life partner to become a good parent! To repair or enhance your adult, committed, intimate relationship, please read Harville Hendrix' classic, *Getting The Love You Want: a guide for couples,* and attend a couples workshop sponsored by the Institute For Imago Relationship Therapy (1-800-729-1121).

Part One

---

*See Who
We Are*

CHAPTER ONE

My Child As A Plant

The plant starts as a
seed. Put it in the ground,
water it, make sure it has just
the right amount of sun and
 nutrients, ...
and it grows!
Not only will it grow,
it will become the
most beautiful plant it can
possibly be. The potential
magnificence of the plant is
contained right in the seed.
 All one needs to do is learn
how to nurture it just the way
 it needs.

THE PLANT

So it is with your children.

They are like plants. Their full potential is already present at birth in their genetic structure. They, like the plants, want to blossom to their full beauty. In order to do that, they must be nurtured in the right way.

MY CHILD (CHILDREN) AS A PLANT
(Instruction: Paste pictures of your children among the plants. Your children are the flowers of the plants!)

Different plants have different needs. Some plants only thrive in a moist environment, others under the heat of the desert sun. Some bloom in the winter months, while others will be killed by the cold.

In order for any specific plant to become the most beautiful plant it can be, we must become familiar with the needs of that particular plant. Once we know what to do in order to care best for that plant, the task becomes a lot clearer. Although it is still a lot of hard work, we know how to <u>direct</u> our hard work toward meeting the needs of the growing plant.

100% chance of failure

Despite our earnest efforts and our good will, sometimes the plant does not thrive. The leaves start turning yellow or begin to droop and fall off.

When that happens we could be tempted to look at the plant disapprovingly, point our finger and say, "Look at you. This is ridiculous! You look awful that way." Or we could hit the plant, or maybe pull on it and stretch it. We could try to shame it into shape. But all we would accomplish that way is to aggravate the situation, and get an even worse looking plant, and an even greater sense of frustration for ourselves.

The only sensible thing to do is to ask ourselves such questions as, "Well, let's see, am I watering this plant enough? or too much? Is it too hot or too cold in this room for that particular plant? Does it get too much direct sunlight? Am I fertilizing it enough?"

In other words, we need to start evaluating the nurturing qualities that we, the caregivers, provide for that plant, because, if we can nurture it just right, the plant will thrive and blossom into its full magnificent potential.

When our children misbehave, they are doing exactly what the plant is doing when it is turning yellow.

or losing its leaves

They are telling us that

something is missing

in the way we care for them.

And, like the plants,

they often don't have the words to express their needs or frustrations.

SO THEY ACT OUT . . . !

Write down the frustrations you currently have with your child. Write the frustration (what your child does that is a problem for you) and then write, "and that frustrates me."

Example:

My child drags bed time on and one until I am completely exhausted. And that frustrates me.

There are many ways our children tell us that despite all our good will and our good intentions, we are not meeting their individual needs. Because their communication is in the form of acting out, you will undoubtedly experience frustration.

List of frustrations I have with my child(ren) - use next page if you need

_____

_____

_____

_____

_____

_____

_____

_____

_____

_____

List of frustrations continued:

_____

_____

_____

_____

_____

_____

_____

_____

_____

_____

_____

_____

_____

WHAT WE HAVE LEARNED SO FAR

The plant always strives to be the most beautiful plant it can be— that's a genetic given. The signs of imperfections that we see are a reflection of the fact that, somehow, the nurturing conditions surrounding the plant are not quite right for that plant— or, that maybe the plant is not the plant of our dreams. Maybe we got a daisy and we were dreaming of a rose.

The same conclusions can be drawn for our children. The misbehaviors we see are their way of telling us that something we are doing is not right for them. Our task as parents or educators is to discover what it is our children need from us, and decipher what they are trying to tell us. Once we understand <u>and act differently</u>, their level of misbehaving will decrease radically to a "normal" human level. None of us is perfect, we never will be, and neither will our children. But we can learn many things about them and do things so differently that their behaviors will become very manageable.

Our children, like living plants, are full of potential and life energy, wanting to burst forth and be all they can be.

CHAPTER TWO

The Way We Were / The Way We Are

Can you remember being a child? Take time to remember. Go back in your imagination to that little person you once were. Settle yourself down, take a deep breath, quiet your spirit, be that child again. Can you remember wanting to please your parents or your teacher? Can you remember so desperately trying to convey to them how much you wanted their approval, how much you wanted them to like you, how desperately you tried to meet their standards and how painful and disappointing it was when you missed the mark?

Take a few minutes to write about some experiences you had of trying hard to please your parents:
"I felt frustrated/angry when . . ."

e.g. 1. I felt frustrated when my mother criticized my table manners.
2. I felt hurt and angry when my father hit my mother in a fight, even though I was trying hard to please him.
3. I felt awful when I studied so hard but still my grades weren't good enough for my parents.

_____

_____

_____

_____

_____

What was your parents' reaction to your attempts to please them and your missing the mark?

Did they scold you? Spank you? Send you to your room? Did they become quiet and refuse to relate to you? What did your parents do when they were displeased with you? Write down what you remember about that:

_____

_____

_____

_____

_____

_____

_____

_____

_____

_____

_____

_____

_____

How did you feel then?

I felt sad. I felt angry. I felt like I would never measure up. I felt inadequate. I felt stupid. I felt that they never understood me. Remember your hurt feelings and write them down.

_____

_____

_____

_____

_____

_____

_____

_____

_____

_____

_____

_____

None of us are perfect (how we wish!). Our parents aren't perfect either— not now nor when we were growing up. They are, and were, good people doing their best at parenting us— probably without ever getting much direction on how to do the task. Consequently, it is most likely that they made some mistakes and that sometimes— or much of the time— you felt hurt and angry.

What are some of the things you wished your parents had done differently? Complete the following sentence:

Mom, Dad (or other name of primary caretaker), what I wish you had done differently is:

_____

_____

_____

_____

_____

If you had done that, I would have felt:

_____

_____

_____

_____

_____

_____

HOW WE PERCEIVE OURSELVES AS ADULTS

The way we feel about ourselves now is directly related to how our parents related to us, and to the fact that, despite their good intentions, they made mistakes.

When I was younger, I used to say, "I am dumb, stupid and ugly," and I believed it totally. I believed I was bad. In fact, I believed I deserved to die.

I no longer feel that way. However, it took me many years to pull myself out of the doldrums.

How about you? How do you feel about yourself? Do you experience yourself as important, lovable, adequate, having something significant to say, to contribute? or do you feel bad, unimportant, ashamed of who you are, frightened that if someone really knew you they would discover what an awful person you really are? What do you truly believe about yourself?

Most of the time, this is what I truly believe about myself:

_____

_____

_____

_____

_____

_____

Which of these statements do you believe about yourself? Circle the ones that apply to you.

"I feel bad about myself, about who I am."
"I do not like myself."
"I am afraid I'm not good enough for my job."
"I am afraid I will be found out as a fake."
"I'm stupid." or "I feel stupid."
"I'm not smart enough."
"I don't believe in myself."
"I am ugly."
"I don't know who I am."
"I don't know what I think, or want."

These are statements of low self-esteem.

Self-esteem, the way we feel about ourselves, and how much we value ourselves, is the result of the quality of the relationship we had with our parents.

As a workshop leader, therapist and educator, I meet many people. By far, the majority often feel bad about themselves. Many people I work with feel inadequate, unimportant and generally unlovable. Chances are this is true for you also. If it isn't true for you, your parenting task will be that much easier and you can be profoundly thankful to your parents who have given you the most wonderful of all gifts, that of feeling good about yourself. It is more unusual, however, to enter adult life with a solid sense of Self, than the other way around.

By and large, our legacy from childhood is the profound notion that we will never measure up. That realization can be so painful that we have to go under cover, hide it from others, and sometimes from ourselves. That's the only way we can survive.

The reason why that happened, is that our parents did not know how to be supportive of our needs. They didn't know how to talk to us, and even more importantly, how to listen. In other words, they didn't know how to provide the right kind of care for the plant they were given. And if that was true of your parents, chances are that it will also be true for you. How could you know something which your parents could never have taught you, since they didn't know it themselves? You can only teach that which you know, and give that which you own.

CHAPTER THREE

Children's Emotional Needs

There are many excellent books that deal with the physical needs and well-being of children. In the following pages, I will focus on their emotional needs.

1. Attachment * (Birth to 18 months)

Attachment is the very first and most profound emotional need that is present at birth. The baby needs to connect with the one caregiver that will be willing to be present as much as possible and answer every need. If a caregiver is reliably present, available and shows great gentleness, warmth, and caring, the child will feel secure. Feeling secure is the bedrock of high self-esteem later in life. Another name for this is bonding. Your task, first and foremost, is to make sure bonding occurs and that there is as little disruption to the connection as possible. **From now on, keeping the connection alive will be your primary guiding light (even into adulthood).**

2. Exploration (18 months to 30 months)

This need starts quite young. The infant in the crib spends fascinating hours discovering that the bundle of flesh that wiggles over there is really her very own foot! As the infant matures into a toddler, the exploratory voyage will expand and include touching, climbing and wanting to run precisely where you just forbade. It is nature's way of helping a child realize he or she is a separate being from the parents.

3. Development of an identity (3-4 years)

There is a strong driving force during these young tender years, as well as during adolescence, to explore various identities from angelic to super powerful to devilish. Let their imagination run

* Harveille Hendrix has identified attachment, exploration, indentity, and competence as the first four stages of development, the most important.

wild! They are becoming increasingly aware of being separate from you. This is the time for no holds barred.

Eventually they'll sort it out if they have been given full permission to try on as many identities as they need.

4. Competence (5-6 years)

As your children learn new skills, they will want to practice them, and they will need you to appreciate those skills and their progress in mastering them.   There is within them a **deep essential need to have their ability valued regardless of their degree of proficiency, because then they know they are valuable.** Our children will value themselves only to the degree that we, the adults in their lives, value them. We are their only source of knowledge with regard to their self-worth. Once they believe in themselves, it becomes as solid as a rock. Self-worth becomes an intricate part of their lives. Once established, it is hard to demolish.

5. Sexuality (from approximately 12 years on)

At puberty, our children will develop sexual needs. We must prepare ourselves early for that so we do not convey a sense of shame around their budding sexuality. Sexuality is an integral aspect of the blossoming of the plant into its most delicately magnificent self.

6. Attention (birth till "death do us part")

Our children need our attention. Lots of it! The less we give them our full attention, the more they need it. Sadly, sometimes, the more they need it, the less we are willing to give it because we experience their need for attention as wrong and irritating. Often it is because we have bought into the "half-empty plate" syndrome. Imagine for a moment your children being hungry. You give them a half portion for fear that if you give them too much food, they will become spoiled and want even more. What would happen then is that they would keep feeling hungry and they would keep whining for more food. If you feed your child until she feels full, then she is no longer hungry and you can all enjoy peace and quiet. Feed your child enough attention, and the hunger will go away. We must begin a journey of believing that, once satiated, our children will no longer be hungry and will be free to move into other directions.

So often, we keep our children emotionally half-starved. Consequently,   they keep begging for more and we end up feeling irritated at them.

7. Respect
There is a deep need in every child to be treated with respect. They need and deserve the same respect we want, and deserve.

Close your eyes for a moment. Think of someone you respect and admire.

Write her or his name here:_____

How would you treat that person in your home?

_____

_____

_____

_____

Our children require the same respect in order to thrive.

8. Feeling Connected

Of the various needs we mentioned: attachment, exploration, identity, competence, sexuality, attention and respect, the greatest need for children is that of <u>feeling</u> attached and <u>feeling</u> connected with their parents.

So, whatever we tell our children, and however we say it, it must be evaluated in this light: "Does it allow my child to still feel connected to me, or does it break the bond?" Because as long as our children feel connected to us, they know they matter to us and they believe in their self-worth. That, in truth, energizes them to do their best.

9. Understanding

What we are all yearning for is understanding. "If mom or dad understands what it's like to be me and is accepting of me regard-less of my performance, then somehow I don't feel so bad about myself, and I can go on." That is the self talk that will go on in your child's head.

It is possible - in fact, imperative - to learn to ask for what we want from them, tell them when they have displeased us <u>and</u> remain compassionate toward them, so that we do not disrupt our bonding with them.

Our task as parents is to be supportive of our children's im-pulses and to learn to say those words that will convey to them that we understand what it is like to be them and that we do not judge the person that they are at that moment, even though we may be displeased with what they've done and we may have to set limits.

The goal, then, is two-fold:

1. Listen to children in such a way as to <u>not place blame or guilt on them</u>.

2. Relate to them in such a way <u>that it does not erode their confidence in themselves.</u>

When you are able to listen and relate, your children will learn that although they may have displeased you, and although they may have missed this or that, they will remain connected with you. They will not experience your love toward them as conditional upon their "perfect" performance. They will know that you do love them just as they are, even though you ask for changes in their behavior, and they will not feel wounded at the core of their being.

Impossible? No, but it is difficult, and it does require practice.

CHAPTER FOUR

A Quick Review

So what have we been saying so far?

1. Children are like plants. All they need to become the most beautiful thriving plant is already present at birth in their genetic material. What they need from <u>you</u> is a nurturing environment in order to blossom.

2. Ain't misbehaving. When the plant is not cared for in just the right way, its leaves turn yellow or drop off. When children do not get their needs met, they "misbehave," act out, or whine. It is their way of telling us that all is not well.

3. Attention. Children's needs include attachment, exploration, identity (including sexual identity for the teen years), competence and . . . an incredible amount of attention . . . unconditional, unabated, focused attention.

Giving them all the attention they need during the first few years is the best insurance against teenage rebellion.

4. We must remain connected with our children at all cost. The attention we give them must be such that it does not blame, does not produce guilt, and ensures that they keep believing in themselves. This way they will feel connected to us and they will feel loved.

The secret is to learn how to -

LISTEN TO THEM!

We can move on to solutions and problem solving only after we have **really listened to them!** Sometimes we are so eager to arrive at solutions, so eager to fix, that we forget to listen. Because we forget to listen, our children cannot experience our love and good will toward them.

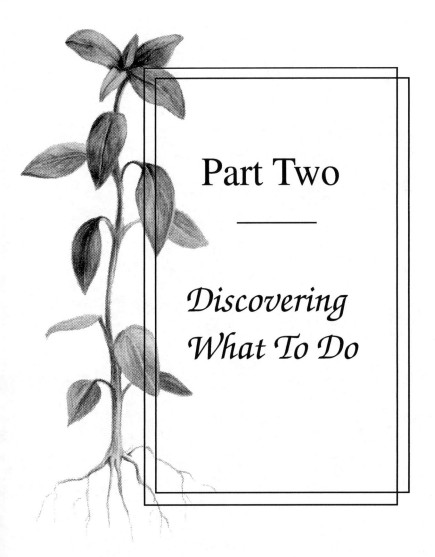

Part Two

---

*Discovering
What To Do*

CHAPTER FIVE

Listening Practice

"The first duty of love is to listen."
— Paul Tillich

Most of us hear quite well what our children are telling us, but few of us know how to listen.

Example:
You were held up by a traffic jam on your way to pick up your daughter from school. You arrive ten minutes late. She is obviously mad at you and says, "Mom, you're always late! I hate to have to wait for you."

Example of a non-listening answer:
"Oh, Honey! I feel awfully bad, but there was an accident on the freeway and I got delayed. Besides, I'm not always late. Usually I'm on time!"

At first glance this could appear to be a fine response. After all, it wasn't "mom's fault" that she was late. It was totally out of her control.

However, this answer was non-listening and therefore non-connecting because it does not let the child know that mom understands how she feels. That's because mom did not remain grounded in her innocence (it <u>was not</u> her fault) and switched the focus away from her daughter's feelings onto her own defense.

So what could mom have said?

Key Concept:
Eliminate the word "but" from your vocabulary. When you say

"but," more than likely something invalidating is coming up.

Key Concept:
Believe in your own innocence. Believe in it so much that you do not have to defend or explain yourself!

Example of a listening answer:
"Honey, it must have felt like I took forever." (Child says, "Yeah!")

"I imagine you might have felt scared waiting for me by yourself like that." (Child says, "Yeah!") "And maybe you were worried we would be late for your practice. " ("Yeah") "I don't blame you. I was worried about that myself."

In this response mom is expressing through her words that she understands her daughter's feelings. Consequently, the child will feel connected, heard, understood and loved.

Key Concept:
Mom doesn't have to defend herself. Even if mom wants to explain what happened, the only way her daughter could hear her is if the connection or bond is intact. If the daughter is angry at mom, mom's explanations will only make matters worse. So, if you absolutely must or want to give an explanation, wait until later and check with your child to make sure he/she is interested. Remember, however, the more you defend yourself, the more you are teaching your child to defend herself.

Another example:
You take your child, Tommy, to the park. Now it is time to go home and he starts whining and saying he doesn't want to leave.

Non listening response:
"Tommy, we have to go home now. Mom has cooked dinner for us! Don't you want to go home and eat? You want to go home and eat Mom's good cooking, don't you?"

Although the child may indeed feel hungry and, therefore,

willingly change his mind, the essence of this response was not that of understanding what it was like to be Tommy. It sounds like dad wanted to go home and was forcing that opinion on Tommy.

What could dad have said?

Listening response:

"Tommy . . . You're having a great time at the park . . . and you don't want to leave. Boy, that makes sense to me . . . I love being at the park with you!

"Hey, Partner! Wouldn't it be fun to stay at the park forever . . . and live in a tree house? Which tree would we choose? That one, huh? Yeah, that looks like a good one.

"Well, Tommy, for now I <u>do</u> want to go home to Mommy. She has prepared dinner for us, and I'm hungry.

"But what do you say we come back next Saturday? Would you like that? How does that sound?"

Now if you make any offer such as this, you must keep your word. Keeping your word will be the cornerstone of building your children's trust.

Of course, I do not know for sure how your children would respond to the listening response I suggested. I'm willing to bet that response would diffuse a lot of the child's disappointment at having to leave the park and would keep the connection alive. It teaches you to stay in relationship with your child while setting your own boundaries; i.e., "I do want to go home. I am hungry." And not something like: "How about we go home now?"

Key Concept:

Keeping the connection alive does not mean that you give in to your children's every demand. It does mean that you validate (not necessarily agree) the reality of their world.

Example:

Your 15-year-old son is discouraged with his report card -

mostly C's and a couple of D's.

Non-listening response:
"No wonder you get these kind of grades. All you do is watch TV or hang around with that crowd which I don't like anyway."

Your son rolls his eyes, goes to his room and slams the door.

"None of that attitude, young man! You're grounded for this weekend!"

You feel hot under the collar, and so does your son. You end up feeling alienated from one another.

Your son does, in fact, spend a lot of time in front of the tube. And it feels legitimate to you that you should shake him up a little.

However, if your goal is to be a source of encouragement for your son so that he can perform at his peak, this is not the right answer. We parents often tend to be teachy and preachy. We become a source of aggravation to our children rather than a source of motivation. Being teachy turns them off!

Isn't that how you felt when your parents would give you their little sermons?

And if that's what your parents did to you, it explains why you might be tempted to use the same approach. Remember, though, if you didn't like it neither will your children, if you use the same approach with them.

If you want to become more conscious, and want to change your pattern of relating to your 15-year-old, this is an example of a listening response.

Listening response:
"Kurt, we just got your report card in the mail. Mom and I would love to sit down with you and look at it together. When would be a good time for you?"

You may think that there would never be a good time for him.

That's because you have not known how to keep it safe for him. He is afraid he is not going to get the respect he wants and deserves.

Let your son know that you are learning a different way of being a parent. And that you will not use this opportunity to pester him.

The following is a respectful way to approach a potentially difficult situation. At the agreed upon time, sit on the couch together. Make sure you are not in a rush (although your son might verbalize that he is!).

The first step is to simply notice the grades: Math - C; English - D; History - D; Physical Education - C; etc.

You read those with a voice that is absolutely neutral. No comments. No "good" or "bad," no "why?" Take a deep breath (make that two!) and remain neutral. Remain grounded. Now is not the time to blow up or punish.

Then ask him, "Well, how do you feel about it, Kurt?"

Non-committal groan.
"Not too sure, eh?"

"It's okay. . . . I guess."

"So it feels fine to you."
(Leave a moment of silence here.)

"I noticed the D in English and in History and I'm wondering if maybe you'd like some help with that."

"It's hard, Dad (Mom). I tried my best."

"Yes, I believe that you tried your best and it <u>really</u> is hard. That's why if you want some extra help, we'd like to be there for you."

"Well, maybe if you could . . ."

Listen to his suggestion. So often our children know exactly what would be helpful to them. Then do all you can to do it, and if that's not possible, offer an alternative that would feel acceptable to all parties involved.

Pointer:

In order to become a source of encouragement to your children, you must remain NEUTRAL. Stay away from blame and/or judgment, including positive judgments, such as, "That's great! You're so good in Math." Consider, instead, using something like, "You seem really happy about your report card. I'm excited for you." - or "You've worked hard and you have good results. You must be very pleased. I appreciate just how hard you've worked."

Question

But what if they're not doing their best?

Stay away from such judgment. Remember, the plant will always strive to be the best plant it can possibly be. It will grow toward the sun. It will fill the space.

So it is with your children. It is quite likely that although it doesn't seem to you that it is their best, chances are it <u>is</u> their best. They simply haven't shared their difficulties and discouragements with you.

Why not?

Because they are afraid of your judgment!

Staying away from any blame and any judgment may be the hardest thing you will ever be asked to do in your life. Keeping your first reaction neutral— away from blame— is absolutely essential to good parenting.

We can only be a source of support for our children if they feel that special connection with us, even if they have messed up— especially when they have messed up. If we are safe for them, they will ask for our advice and for direction from us. That's the time to give it, not before.

Feeling safe with us, knowing that we won't reject them, shame them or humiliate them even when they have erred— that's the meaning of love. Love for our children needs to be unconditional. That is what we want to strive for. Only then will they do their best.

So, the essence of a listening response is that it does not judge, blame, explain things away or try to fix. Instead, it reflects back the emotional content of what the child was saying with warmth and caring — **even if we disagree or are displeased.** Be aware, the more you disagree or are displeased, the harder it will be to stay neutral. You may need to take some time off for yourself, a cooling off period, or regain your emotional balance. And if you lose it, well, apologize and start again.

I will tell you later how to ask your children to change their behaviors. But before the children can hear you on that, you must first hear them. Because they are the children and you are the parents, the burden of listening falls on you.

Only as you listen to them, will they learn to listen to you! Furthermore, they will listen to you only to the degree that you listen to them.

As the parent, you are called upon to have a mature reaction first. It is very hard to do and you have the right to feel frustrated. Share your frustration with a friend, with your partner, with your counselor or your consultant, not with your children.

It is not the role of children to be our confidants.

Later in this handbook I will suggest that you start a neighborhood PIP Group (Partners In Parenting Group), which I mentioned earlier. That's the place to share your frustrations at the annoying behavior of your children!

When we learn to listen and reflect back with warmth and empathy what our children say to us, we build a bridge between our children and ourselves.

The bridge keeps the connection alive.

COLORADO BOULEVARD BRIDGE , PASADENA , CALIFORNIA —

The girders of the bridge are:

1. Listen

2. Reflect back

3. Empathize

CHAPTER SIX

The Wall

When we blame, judge, criticize, or give unasked-for advice, we create a wall between ourselves and our children.

When we use "but," "I know," "I understand," or ask "why?" we become attacking, and more stones are added to the wall.

"Whys" often put one on the defensive and they violate one's privacy. These are some of the stones that build the wall.

Wall Building
When we do not allow our children to express what they feel, we erect walls between us. Then we lose our connection.

Are you surprised to see "reassuring" on the wall? I was.

Let's assume you just got the results of a biopsy that indicates that you have cancer. A well-meaning friend says to you, "Don't worry, they really have cancer under control these days. The new treatments work so much better than ever before. My mom has just been given a clean bill of health. I'm sure you'll be okay. Think positive."

Now compare this to a friend who would say, "My, you must be really worried. Would you like to tell me about it?"

You probably will feel more connected with the friend who gives you the second response. That friend acknowledges your worries and honors your fear. You are a little bit less alone, now that someone understands what it's like to be you and honors it, respects it, and does not shame you for your fears and concerns.

That's what our children need from us: a safe person who honors and respects what it's like to be who they are. "Being me isn't quite so painful or so shameful if mom and dad understand me."

And the way you, mom and dad, can show that you understand them, is by reflecting back warmly and empathically, **the emotional content** of what you hear— whether or not you agree with the actual content and whether or not you have a solution. The goal is not to fix. The end product is not really as important as the process of connecting with your child.

Example of Empathic Statements:

"You must be feeling worried."

"I imagine you're mad about that!"

"That must be so frustrating!"

"I would guess it hurts to lose such a good friend."

CHAPTER SEVEN

Listening Responses - Your Turn

Now that you understand the general concepts, it is time for you to practice.

Example:
Your 2-year-old son gets frightened by the thunder. He comes running to you, crying.

What might you have told your son before you started working with this handbook? Get in touch with that and write it down.

A non-listening response:
You pick him up and say:

_____

_____

_____

_____

_____

_____

Now, go back to "The Wall" and see if you can identify why the above answer is a non-listening answer. It builds a wall because it is _____.(name the stones)

Now, give a listening response. You can write your listening response with a consultant if you wish or with one of your PIP Group members.

50

A listening response:
You pick him up and say:

_____

_____

_____

_____

_____

Example:
Your 18-year-old daughter is worried because she hasn't been invited yet to a major dance on campus, still a month away.

A non-listening response:

_____

_____

_____

_____

_____

_____

Checking "The Wall," state why this is a non-listening response.

_____

_____

_____

_____

_____

_____

A listening response:

_____

_____

_____

_____

_____

_____

Example

When your 13-year-old son (whose grades are barely passing) wants to skateboard after school till dark, you firmly tell him no. He slams the door to his room, yelling, "I hate you! All you want to do is control me and keep me in this stupid house like a prisoner. None of my friends' parents are like you!"

A non-listening response:

_____

_____

_____

_____

_____

Check "The Wall." State why this is a non-listening response.

_____

_____

_____

_____

_____

A listening response:

_____

_____

_____

_____

Turn to page 68 to see how I filled out this chapter. Compare it with your answers.

But, you may ask, how do I give a listening response when my child is too young to talk?

The following, originally printed in "Mothering" magazine a while back, is the most beautiful answer I can possibly give you.

One Angry Night
by Leenie Hobbie

My three-day-old daughter taught me more about anger in one night than I had learned in all 31 years of my life. As she raged and hollered and demanded to be heard, I responded as I had learned all good mothers should. I patted, I walked, I rocked, I soothed, I massaged, and I "It's OK, baby" -ed until utter helplessness overcame me. She was healthy, strong, dry, warm, safe . . . and still she raged. I meditated with her in my arms; I visualized; and I cried. She, all the while, continued to holler.

In a desperate burst of inspiration, I held her in front of me, cradled in my arms. I looked deeply into her eyes— not as a mother trying to soothe her babe, but as a fellow human being trying to find her way on this planet. Suddenly, I began to feel her anger. I gave up my search for causes and solutions, and simply acknowledged her feelings: "Right on, Sister! Tell it like it is! Yes, Sister! Word up! Speak out, Little Sister!"

She stopped, stunned. Staring at me with red-rimmed eyes, she looked deeply into my eyes. She shut her puffy lids and let out one more powerful yell. Feeling her rage, I offered encouragement once again. Then, with abandon, she sank into the haven of my arms. No more stiffness. No more resistance.

We became one in understanding. She knew she was appreciated and could count on being heard. I knew we were more than our roles implied: we were two human beings united through compassion and respect. Ever since that night, we have both slept peacefully through the hours of darkness.

The answer of course, was that this mother eventually stopped trying to "fix" her infant thus conveying that something was wrong with her, and embraced an attitude of full respect and acceptance for the person of the child, regardless of her screaming and in spite of her disress. This mother became a listening mother when she stopped trying to control and empathically moved toward understanding.

CHAPTER EIGHT

Solutions

Congratulations for your commitment in working with the previous exercises. It is likely that by now you have used reflective listening with your children. And if you have, I am absolutely convinced that you have already experienced a decrease in tension between you and your children.

Keep reflecting back.

Keep stretching and stretching to really see where the children are coming from. <u>Even if you disagree with them.</u>

Even though you may disagree with what they <u>did,</u> validate their <u>feelings.</u>

"I can imagine that little Susie makes you awfully angry— always trying to play with <u>your</u> toys. It makes sense to me that you are feeling frustrated right now. Would you like to show me how angry you feel? You can show me by pounding on the bed, kicking the ball, or by scribbling with your crayons on the board, or on this paper. Which would you like to do? " (Whenever possible, give them choices.)

Yet, if Billy does hit Susie or if Susie does not stop harassing Billy, you will feel the need for some solutions. But before you can arrive at any solution, you have to know how to listen with hour heart.

There are ways of asking your children to change their behaviors with minimum disruption of the connection between you. Spanking, time-out, and other forms of punishment are <u>not</u> on the list.

WHY PUNISHMENT IS OUT
Punishment is out because:

1. It does not insure that the misbehavior will not be repeated; in fact, it is almost guaranteed you will have to dish out the punishment over and over again.

2. It gives the adult a false sense of security.

3. It is humiliating for the child.

4. Since children crave attention, they may repeat a misbehavior just to get attention, even negative attention.

5. Punishment breaks the bond.

6. Through punishment our children learn that "they are bad". If our children end up believing they are bad, they might as well misbehave. It almost always becomes a self-fulfilling prophecy.

This is the self-talk of the misbehaving child:
"You think I'm bad; therefore, I know I'm bad. So, being bad or acting bad is natural for me. It is who I believe I am."

The learning we want our children to do can only be done in an atmosphere of love and respect. Remember the person you respect and whose name you wrote down on page 31. You have to respect your child to that same degree.

7. Out of punishment comes rebellion and a desire for vengeance, even though initially it may produce compliance. Under enough pressure, children will give us the illusion of compliance, that is, doing as we wish. But it is only an illusion— an illusion of power for the parents because the child is doing as he or she is told. After ten to fifteen years, this system will break down. Witness the flourishing activities of gangs and the rampant use of drugs and various addictions in all segments of society.

We need to devise a system that feels respectful and empowering to our children <u>as well as</u> respectful to ourselves.

Family Round Table

I would like to propose that you establish a weekly family meeting, which I call the "Family Round Table," and I will tell you how to conduct this meeting in Chapter 9.

Decide for now what day and time would work best for you. It should be from 30 minutes to 1 hour, depending on the ages of your children. Mark it on your calendar and treat it as a nost important appointment. It is as sacred and necessary as feeding your children.

I would like us to meet on_____

from_____ to _____

CHAPTER NINE

The Family Round Table

Announce to your family that you want to start a new way of cooperating as a family and that this will require a special time together: a weekly Family Round Table. Give everyone a piece of paper to write their preferred day and time, in the same way you wrote your preferred day and time in the previous chapter.

Your children may sigh and roll their eyes, conveying to you, "Oh no, not one of those dumb meetings!" If that happens, my recommendation is that you say the following:

"We've had family meetings in the past, and they haven't been fun, have they? I think in the past I made you feel that we had these meetings to hassle you. So I can imagine you wouldn't be looking forward to that. I am committed to doing things totally differently."

Come to the best compromise possible with regard to day and time of the meeting, and as a parent, remember to walk the extra mile! Tell your children you are going to teach them how to solve problems together.

The Agenda
Tell your family that you have a clipboard, paper and pencil in the den (or any central place that works for your home) and that whenever a problem comes up for someone during the week, each person will write it on the agenda (or if they're too young, write it for them). This will allow for a period of disengagement, a time for cooling off. It will help you to stay detached and "let the dust settle." It will also begin to build up a list of problems that have come up during the week. That list becomes your agenda for your Family Round Table.

By the time the meeting comes up, you may be surprised that some of the issues will have become "non issues." All the better!

Staying out of the children's quarrels and freeing yourself from problem-solving when you are still hot under the collar is a process I call <u>containment.</u> Successful parenting requires that you learn the skill of containment. Containment does not mean ignoring the problems. It means that you are willing to wait for a more appropriate time that will be more productive.

Example:
16 year-old Mary stays out until midnight. Her curfew is 10 pm. Today is Tuesday. The family meeting is on Sunday. What to do?
You might state, "I feel upset about what happened last night." THAT'S ALL! Don't preach, don't explode. Hold it in. Talk to your spouse if you have one or call a member of your PIP Group if you have one (and I hope you do!)

When you are in the middle of your reaction, nothing constructive can happen. Better put it on the agenda of the Family Round Table and deal with it in the agreed upon manner.

Remember, as you learn to fully respect your children, they, too, will learn to respect you and your teenager will be less likely to misbehave. However, it all takes time.

The Family Round Table

When the time comes for your Family Round Table, respect it fully. Nothing can come up to disrupt it.

Sit around a table. You be the chairperson the first week in order to get started. After that, rotate the chairperson. Explain that to the rest of the family. Explain to your family that the chairperson will be responsible for the following:

1) Making sure the Family Round Table starts with everyone taking a turn to thank each person for at least one thing that person did during the week.

Suppose one family member refuses to participate? Reflect back what that person said and you may want to put it on the agenda for the next week. Wait patiently (no preaching) until everyone has thanked everyone else. Remain silent as you wait.

2) Making sure that only one person speaks at a time and that the person talking will finish what they have to say.

Example: "Diane, Billy wasn't finished yet. Please wait until he's done. Thanks."

3) Making sure everyone understands that this is a time to put heads together to design a solution to the problem that is mutually acceptable to all. The goal is not a "perfect" solution; rather, one that everyone can live with.

Explain, as well, that the Family Round Table is <u>not a time for:</u>
- Punishment!
- Teachy/Preachy Moralizing
- Judgment
- Shaming
- Nagging

The Family Round Table is a time to set boundaries and make requests of one another, in a manner that is firm and kind and respectful.

The problems will be addressed in the order they come up on the agenda you have been building all week. After the person who wrote the first item explains the problem thoroughly, and you, as the parent, reflect back to make sure you fully understand your child, open up the discussion for suggestions to resolve the issue currently being addressed. MAKE SURE YOU FULLY UNDER-

STAND YOUR CHILD'S PERSPECTIVE FIRST BEFORE YOU MOVE ON. Rushing this part would undermine the rest of your time together. And remember you will not agree! You are still to remain neutral and warm.

Write down every suggestion, no matter how outrageous or seemingly unfeasible it seems to you. Do not censor any, or it could give your child the impression that something is wrong with him/her since his/her suggestion was eliminated immediately. In fact, I recommend that you, yourself, start with an outrageous suggestion. That will give your children permission to do the same.

Every single suggestion is worth writing down and all family members, regardless of age, are encouraged to make their own suggestions and share their ideas regardless of the apparent feasibility of the suggestion.

IN YOUR FAMILY
EVERYONE WILL HAVE A VOICE
AND
EVERY VOICE WILL BE HEARD

Finding Solutions

The solutions arrived at must feel reasonable from the perspective of both parent(s) and child and the whole process must be respectful. After everyone has an opportunity to share his/her ideas, go over the list of suggestions and eliminate (put a line through) those that are totally out of the question for any single member of the family.

Keep repeating the process until you are all willing to try one solution.

The solution must be arrived at by consensus. It may not be perfect for anyone, but it must be a solution all agree they can live with at least for the coming week. Remember, you are the parent. Model walking the extra mile for your children.

Example 1:
Problem:
Mom: "Daryl's bedroom is too messy. I can't even change the sheets or vacuum and it is not acceptable to me."

The first step is to ask Daryl, "Would you be willing to tell me about how difficult it is to keep your bedroom clean and help me understand that?"
Listen. Reflect back. Show warmth and empathy. Take time to really understand. Then say,
"Thank you, Daryl, for explaining how it is for you. Thank you. What do you suggest we could do to resolve this problem between us?"

Now you build a list of possible solutions. It could look something like this:

- Keep my bedroom door closed and don't ever come in.

- Make your bed and pick up your clothes every day before you go to school.

- Pick up your clothes once a week.

- We will hire a maid.

- Change bed sheets once a week.

- Once during the weekend, child will change sheets, pick up clothes and vacuum.

- Mom will change the sheets and do the vacuuming after clothes are off the floor and in their proper place.

- Mom and child will change sheets together after the clothes are picked up. Mom will do the vacuuming once a week during the weekend, or maybe child will do the vacuuming.

After everyone has shared his/her own ideas as to possible solutions, go back and cross out any solution that is absolutely not acceptable to either you or your daughter/son. You will be left with some possibilities that you will negotiate together, with kindness and mutual respect.

Example 2:

I recently met with a mom and her 14-year-old daughter. They are committed to using the principles of the Family Round Table. They both report having a tendency to procrastinate and yet love the results when they do discipline themselves to have a Family Round Table. Every once in a while they come to me for coaching.

Today, the issue at hand was mom's upset with Melody's make up (not her real name). The first step was, of course, to really listen to one another. Eventually Melody explained, "I don't like to disobey you but I couldn't possibly go out with a friend without some make up. She would be gorgeous and I would feel so unattractive and 'dorky.' At one level, I don't want to disobey you, at another level, I fell so needy that I just feel better about myself when I wear make up."

Those words resonated with such depth in both mom and myself. Nothing could have ever let mom know how badly Melody feels about herself. Outwardly she is intelligent, articulate, talented, and very pretty. From our adults' perspective, she has the word "success" written all over her.

It was profoundly touching to hear her say she felt badly about herself, ugly, insecure. Even though she does not prefer to disobey her mother, still she would because the idea of going out without make up is even more unbearable.

The decision they arrived at that day was that melody was going to put on make up in a way that felt reasonable to her and mom would give her feedback. Melody then agreed that those would be the guidelines she would follow when putting on make up.

There remained one issue, that of Melody calling mom to ask for permission before wearing make up. We ran out of time. That had to be tabled.

The next time we met, mom talked about her concern about Melody's desire to wear make up. At first she talked about her fear that Melody would be kidnapped. As Melody mirrored and tried to understand her mother's concern, it emerged that the real issue was sexuality. They had an open dialogue about the dangers of becoming sexually active too young which was mom's personal history. It was again the work of two very mature, good willed individuals learning to really listen to what each had to say.

You may worry that all of this takes too long. And yes, at one level it does take time to get through even one issue. Yet it is also a more efficient way than the numerous and recurring yelling matches they had had about these issues in the past.

Eventually, mom didn't feel the need to be called first about wearing make up. Their open communication helped build trust in her. If and when Melody were to abuse the privilege of wearing make up, they would be willing to put it on the agenda again. But until then, mom is going to trust.

I find it so gratifying two human beings beginning to understand each other, to discuss a difficult topic with an open mind and a sincere desire to find a solution to pave the way in a spirit of generosity and understanding. That is what the Family Round Table is all about.

Pointers:

An attitude of mutual respect will foster cooperation.

At first your children will most likely test you, test your good will, push you to see if you really mean it. That is normal. Just be prepared and know that, most likely, it will happen.

Remain calm. If you think you are about to "lose it," ask for a break for yourself. Go take a drink, take a few deep breaths, and regain your centeredness.

This is a tremendous learning experience for parents! With practice you <u>CAN</u> do it.

Now, you have come up with a solution for the coming week. Because children are children, because learning new patterns is difficult to do, don't expect a miracle. Your children will test you. Put the issue back on the agenda. Keep working through your problems as a family in that fashion. If you do it with kindness and consistency, you will break the power struggle between you and your children. But remember, change takes time for you as well as your children.

You must make a commitment to yourself to say nothing to your child about his or her commitment. Now your task is to trust.

Don't nag, don't remind them. If the task wasn't done, put it up on the agenda for the next meeting. At that time, listen first as to why it wasn't done. Really take the time to understand. Reflect back and empathize. Go back to find a mutually acceptable solution. Do that calmly, kindly, and with a respectful firmness.

With time and adherence to these guidelines, your children will learn both self-discipline and co-operation and in this manner, all family members will feel empowered.

HELPFUL HINTS

1. Practice detachment.
    Detachment is when you can hold back your thoughts on the topic at hand, control your emotions for the moment, stay out of the loop and remain neutral. I also call this "containment." It will help to have your PIP Group with whom you can share your frustrations!

2. Develop an attitude of cooperation with your children.

In your relationship with them, make it a habit to start by focusing on really understanding <u>their</u> world, what it's like to be them. Get "into" their skin!

3. Remain kind, warm, respectful, and non-punitive in spirit.

If you learn to really listen to your children, to hold back <u>your</u> thoughts in order to hear theirs,

If you learn to really listen with your heart, focusing on the meaning your children are trying to convey to you,

If you focus on preserving the bond between you,

it will create a climate of safety for your children.

Rather than being afraid of you, which invites lying, they will feel safe with you. Then, they <u>will feel</u> your love and they will learn that they are lovable. They will value themselves because you value their opinion. They will feel cherished even when their behavior has to be limited.

Then, they will be able to tap into their core life force, and they will blossom into the magnificent people they really are!

How I filled out pages 49 to 52.

1. Frightened by the thunder (p. 49-50)

A non-listening response: Pick him up and say, "It's okay sweetie. There is nothing to be afraid of. It's just the thunder. It's okay." — and you pat him on his back.

The Wall: reassurance

A listening response: "My . . . that was a BIG noise! . . . really scary . . . yeah. You felt really afraid. I like it when you come and tell Mommy when you're afraid."

Later, as your child calms down and feels better you might ask, "Would you like Mommy to tell you what happened?" Act according to the child's response.

2. Hasn't been invited to the dance (p. 50-51)

A non-listening response: "Well, honey don't be so impatient. There is still plenty of time to be invited. Don't worry, you're very attractive. I'm sure everything will turn out okay."

The Wall: Criticism; un-asked for advice; reassurance.

A listening response: "I can imagine that you feel worried about that. It would feel awful not to be invited. Tell me more about your worries."

3. 13 year old who isn't allowed to skateboard after school (p. 51-52)

A non-listening response: "Well, if you think that kind of attitude is going to get you anywhere, you have another one coming. And, I'm not going to let you talk to me like that."

The Wall: teachy/preachy; criticism; judgment

A listening response: "You really think that my rules are unfair and you feel very angry at me right now. That makes sense to me. It makes sense to me that you would rather go skateboarding. Right now I don't want to let you do that."

Part Three

Forming
PIP Groups
(Partners In Parenting Groups)

CHAPTER TEN

Forming PIP Groups
(Partners In Parenting Groups)

YOUR FIRST PIP GROUP MEETING

I am hoping that you have agreed with friends, and/or neighbors, to meet together weekly and explore your parenting journey together.

Before you begin, it is important that you establish some ground rules everyone is willing to abide by.

STEP ONE: Decide on your meeting schedule.
Will you meet once a week or every other week? (no less) Where will you meet? For how long will you meet? No less than one hour is recommended, but if you only have a half hour lunch break, go   for it.

STEP TWO: Only one person talks at a time.
Each person should share without interruption. During a person's sharing, there should be no questions, no "that's terrible," "that's wonderful," "me too," or "really?" Each group member commits to holding inside any reactions to the sharing. That kind of personal discipline is one of the cornerstones of effective parenting, and is the true meaning of "support."

STEP THREE: Mirror back first.
Before the next person shares, the group will mirror back what that first person said; each person mirrors a piece of it, and says, "thank you for sharing that with us." After everything has been mirrored back, the next person is now ready to share.

You will want to exchange phone numbers, as well, in case you need extra support during the week.

STEP FOUR: Commit to confidentiality.
Hear yourself say the following to other group members:
"Kathy, Tom, Bonnie, and Mary, what you will tell me in this PIP Group will be kept in total confidentiality. I make a commitment to all of you that I will not betray your trust."

And do that! Do not talk about group matters outside the group <u>under any circumstances</u>!

End your first meeting with a meditation on the work of loving your children. Read the following quote out loud to each other:

"For one human being to love another human being: that is perhaps the most difficult task that has been entrusted to us, the ultimate task, the final test and proof, the work for which all other work is merely preparation."
- Rainer Maria Rilke, <u>*Letters to a Young Poet*</u>

Then each member tells the other members of the group:
"Thank you for being willing to work with me in the difficult task of loving my child(ren) and thank you for letting me be a part of your work of loving your children."

In the following seven chapters, I have presented seven modules for your PIP Group to work through. Each module may take several group sessions. Don't rush yourselves. Doing each module thoroughly is more important than pushing your way through them all quickly. Learning and change can only come slowly.

Before the first meeting of each module, do <u>Part 1: To do alone</u> first. Also bring a picture of your child(ren) to the very first PIP Group meeting.

CHAPTER ELEVEN

PIP Group Module One
- Acceptance -

. . . You may give them your love, but not your thoughts
for they have their own thoughts
You may house their bodies but not their souls
for their souls dwell in the house of tomorrow
which you cannot visit, not even in your dreams.
You may strive to be like them,
but seek not to make them like you.

- Kahlil Gibran, *The Prophet*

Out of our pain emerges our potentially greatest stumbling block along the journey of parenthood: accepting our children as they are. Often we want them different— bigger, better, more of this, less of that. We want to create them "in our image" which we think is a better version than who they are.

In this module, you will work on accepting the plant you have been given. Remember that it is a process and it does not happen overnight. Be gentle with yourself. Most especially, be patient and appreciate every step you're taking, no matter how small it may look to you.

Part 1 - To Do Alone

Take some time now to reflect on the idea of your child as a plant that already possesses everything it needs to blossom into the most wonderful, most perfect specimen it can possibly be and that may be very different from what your best friend has. I hope you have affixed a photo of each of your children on page 14 of this handbook. If not, do it now. Study their sweet faces as you ponder and write your honest responses to the following questions, repeating the exercise for each child:

In what ways is this child not the kind of "plant" I hoped for?

What aspects of his or her physical appearance have been a disappointment to me, or different from what I expected? Consider things like gender, eye color, hair color or texture, skin color, shape of face and body, height and weight. Please be specific and elaborate. Feel free to use another sheet of paper, if necessary.

_____

_____

_____

_____

What character traits of this child have been difficult for me to accept, or different from what I expected? Is he or she too boisterous or quiet, not as affectionate as I'd like, too dependent or independent, more serious or too lighthearted? Please be specific and elaborate.

_____

_____

_____

_____

What about this child's interests and achievements have been different from what I hoped for? Is he or she more or less intelligent than I hoped for, too artistic, not athletic enough, not motivated enough, too competitive, less social? Please be specific and elaborate.

_____

_____

_____

_____

_____

_____

Was this child planned? Or would I have liked to have waited a little longer, or not had the child at all? Please be specific and elaborate.

_____

_____

_____

_____

_____

_____

Perhaps you were not quite ready yet when this child came into your life. Perhaps you dreamed of a child who would be vastly different, who would share your interests or achieve things that you had never been able to achieve for yourself. Let yourself acknowledge these things. Give yourself permission to feel the sadness, the disappointment, the anger, the frustration, and the resentment of being given a plant that is so very different from what you had dreamed of. Let go of any guilt or judgment. There is no one to be blamed. If you can feel the sadness and move away from guilt and blame, you will be energized for change.

Part 2 - Your Week In Review

Go around the room and share with the group the successes and frustrations you have had with your children during the past week. Especially, talk about your Family Round Table. How is it going? If you haven't started yet, I urge you to do so.

Make sure every speaker gets mirrored by the group and that listeners do not fall into the trap of "fixing" or "problem-solving."

After you have all shared, move on to Part 3.

Part 3 - Sharing With Your PIP Group

Now you will share Part 1 of this exercise and benefit from your group's support and validation. Choose one person to share (the speaker). The group will listen and repeat back what the speaker has shared without making any interpretations. This is called mirroring.

A mirror does not agree nor disagree, nor does it make an evaluation. It simply reflects back the sun rays that hit its surface.

The first speaker will read what she has written in Part I, one paragraph at a time. After each paragraph, she will pause. The group will reflect back (mirror) what was said, <u>without adding anything</u> and then will thank the speaker for sharing.

For example:
Speaker #1, Sharon, reads:

"My child, Timmy, is not the kind of plant I'd hoped for because I had really been wishing for a little girl. I didn't like his looks at all in the beginning. He didn't look anything like my side of the family."

Listener #1, Marcia, mirrors:

"So what you're saying, Sharon, is that Timmy is not the kind of plant you'd hoped for because you had really been wishing for a little girl. Thank you."

Sharon nods or says yes. (If the listener has repeated something incorrectly, the speaker should repeat the sentence and the listener should re-mirror and re-verify until it has been mirrored correctly.)

Listener #2, Laura, mirrors:

"And you said that you didn't like his looks at all in the beginning. Thank you."

Listener #3, Donna, mirrors:

"And, also, he didn't look anything like your side of the family. Thank you."

Continue in this manner until Speaker #1 has shared everything she's written. Then she will become one of the listeners for the next person. The listeners are to hold back any comment, agreement or disagreement, or identification with what the speaker is saying. The goal is always to remain supportive <u>and</u> neutral. No matter how strong the urge may be to exclaim, "You feel that way too? That's exactly how I feel about my Tiffany!" - **don't do it!** Although this type of response may seem supportive, it actually takes the focus off the speaker and puts it onto the listener. <u>It is imperative that the focus remain on the speaker until her turn is completed.</u> Hold each listener strictly to mirroring and validating what's been said and nothing more. For, if we cannot learn to focus on one another, we will never be able to do so with our children. As you continue to practice, this way of communicating will become easier and more natural. This form of mirroring as a group is called **group mirroring**. No one person mirrors it all.

Some definitions:

Mirroring: Mirroring is when you have an agreement with someone to repeat back to them word for word what they said. This is a powerful way to let the sender know that they are being taken seriously and heard accurately.

Group Mirroring: Group mirroring is when all members of the group repeat back to the sender small pieces of what was said. They keep taking turns until everything is repeated. After each turn, the one who mirrors will say, "Thank you for sharing."

Reflecting back: This is when a parent reflects back to a child the emotional content of what was said. Reflecting back is not word for word mirroring. An example of this is when Johnny comes home discouraged and says, "I hate my teacher. She picks on me and makes me feel stupid." You say, "It really feels unfair." You use "reflecting back" when you do not have an agreement for word for word mirroring such as with a neighbor or friend.

Part 4 - Meditation

Now, look again at the photo(s) of your child(ren). As you study each of their faces, read the following meditation out loud:

You are my very special plant— the plant that

has been given to me so that I can learn how to nurture. There is no other exactly like you. My sole task is to discover the kind of plant you are and the kind of nurturing you need in order to blossom into your fullest potential. As I look at your face, I can truly see the wonder of this gift which the universe, in its infinite wisdom, has selected just for me. And although you are not what I thought you would be, or even hoped you would be, I can now see that you are perfectly, magnificently, precisely as you are supposed to be. And as I learn to release my expectations, as I learn to be sensitive to your needs and become an agent for your growth, you will open to me joyfully and lovingly, as the daisy opens to the morning sun. Today, I dedicate myself to this journey. Today, I dedicate myself to loving you in the way you need to be loved.

You may not all have time to finish everything today. That's okay. Take the next week to finish, or as many weeks as it takes. What is important is that, eventually, each of you will share the way in which your child has not been the kind of plant you had hoped for.

Part 5 - To Do At Home

Immediately after meeting with your PIP Group, return to a private place in your home and repeat the meditation in Part 4 of this exercise. Repeat this meditation regularly.

CHAPTER TWELVE

PIP Group Module Two
- Remembering Your Pain -

Reading about a wonderful new technique does not make us emotionally capable of integrating the new behavior— even if it is our fondest desire to do so. There are stronger, much more deeply ingrained forces at work, namely the emotional pain we experienced as children.

This pain must be reckoned with if we are ever to have the kind of relationship with our children that we have always dreamed of.

". . . family pain broke us open and set our hearts on a pilgrimage in search of love and belonging, safety and abundance, joy and peace that were missing from our childhood story. Seen through this lens, family sorrow is not only a painful wound to be endured, analyzed, and treated. It may, in fact, become a seed that gives birth to our spiritual healing and awakening"

— Wayne Muller, *The Legacy of the Heart*

Being raised by parents who are human and are themselves the product of human parents— splintered by their fears, trapped by their insecurities and limited by their knowledge— it would only make sense that you, too, have been caught in a cycle of imperfection that resulted in your experiencing some form of pain.

Part 1: To Do Alone

This week let yourself experience some of the pain that undoubtedly came your way as a youngster. Despite their love for you, your parents made mistakes; in order to become the parents you envision, it is important that you feel compassion and tenderness for the little child <u>you</u> once were.

Can you remember an event that really hurt? It may have been at school, being teased by classmates or humiliated by a teacher. It may have been at home, misunderstood by Mom and Dad. Punished unfairly. Bullied by siblings.

Write down the event as you remember it.

_____

_____

_____

_____

_____

How did it make you feel?

Sad - Angry - Lonely - Abandoned - Rejected - Scared

Ashamed - Guilty - Misunderstood - Unappreciated

Circle what you felt or write your own feelings.

_____

_____

_____

_____

_____

Because we are the product of a world that has usually denied and under-estimated children's capacity to feel, you may have a difficult time knowing how you felt. That's okay. In time, you will begin to re-connect with your feelings and your pain.

If you are unable to re-connect with your feelings, when it is your time to share, simply say, "I'm not sure how that made me feel . . ." or "It was so long ago . . . I don't know."

Part 2 - Your Week In Review

Just as in the last module, share and have a group mirror of both successes and difficulties you encountered this past week.

Part 3 - Sharing With Your PIP Group

Do this exactly as described in Chapter 11.

Part 4 - Meditation - To Tell the Group Out Loud

I have been hurt. I have felt angry. I have experienced rejection, oppression and judgment. But I will not let my pain interfere with the parent I want to be. I am committed to transforming these unpleasant feelings into a kind of positive energy, that will gently move me toward personal growth and healing.

Thank you _____ for being willing to
              (group member's name)

walk beside me on my journey.

Again, this module may take more than one meeting to complete. Take all the time it takes for all of you to re-visit your childhoods and to share some sad highlights with each other in a caring environment.

CHAPTER THIRTEEN

PIP Group Module Three
- Letting Go -

"Few of us have been so generously parented ourselves that we have the ability to be truly selfless in our giving . . . In fact, many of us arrive at the portal of parenthood so badly deprived of parenting . . . so filled with fears and insecurities that as a consequence we want to possess and control."

- Daphne Rose Kingman, *A Garland of Love*

Relinquishing control— that is perhaps the greatest lesson our children have to teach us. To give up our dreams for our children to be the way that we want them to be, in order to cherish them just as they are; to celebrate the mystery that they embody; to grasp the deep essence of their uniqueness— that will stretch us to our limits, and, paradoxically, at the same time, enable us to grow.

Part 1 - To Do Alone

Did your parents use control when you were a child? And if so, how? Did they coerce or pressure you? Did they impose their will on you? Did they make you feel guilty?

Write what you remember about that.

_____

_____

_____

_____

When your parents wanted to control you, did they use punishment? What kind of punishment? (circle what applies)

Spanking - Shaming me - Sending me to my room

Grounding me - or?

_____

Did they give you a reward when they liked what you did?

What kind of rewards did they use?

_____

_____

_____

_____

Did your parents let you get away with murder? If so, how did that feel?

_____

_____

_____

_____

Part 2 - Your Week In Review
Follow the format in the previous module.

Part 3 - Sharing With Your PIP Group
Share the material from Part 1 with your group in the manner outlined before.

Part 4 - Meditation

The following poem has been helpful to me. I have made a few minor changes, and I read it over and over to remind myself that <u>my</u> task is to "let go." Read it out loud to each other. I hope it will be a source of personal challenge for you as it is for me.

LETTING GO

To "let go" does not mean to stop caring about you,
*   it means I can't do it for you.*
To "let go" is not to cut myself off from you,
*   it is the realization I can't control you.*
To "let go" is not to enable you,
*   but to allow you to learn from natural consequences.*
To "let go" is to admit my powerlessness,
*   which means the outcome is not in my hands.*
To "let go" is not to try to change or blame you,
*   it is to make the most of myself.*
To "let go" is not to care for,
*   but to care about you.*
To "let go" is not to fix you,
*   but to be supportive of you.*
To "let go" is not to judge you,
*   but to allow you to be a human being.*
To "let go" is not to be in the middle arranging all the outcomes,
*   but to allow you to affect your own destiny.*
To "let go" is not to be protective of you,
*   it's to permit you to face reality.*
To "let go" is not to deny,
*   but to accept you.*
To "let go" is not to nag, scold or argue,
*   but instead to search out my own shortcomings and correct them.*
To "let go" is not to adjust everything to my desires
*   but to take each day as it comes, and cherish myself in it.*
To "let go" is not to regret the past,
*   but to grow and live for today.*
To "let go" is to fear less and love you more.

                                                    - Author Unknown

Part 5 - To Do At Home

When you are at home and your child(ren) are asleep, gently read the poem to them and personalize it. It would look like this:

To "let go" does not mean that I stop caring <u>about you</u>, Jimmy, it means that I can't do it for you.

To "let go" is not to cut myself off <u>from you, Jimmy</u>, it's the realization, I can't control you....... and so forth.

You may want to add the following:

<u>Shelly,</u> I do not want to be intrusive in your life or coerce you. That would only create temporary obedience and develop resentment in you.

I want to work with you, I want to believe in you, I want to have faith in you, I want to respect you.

I want to give you as much freedom as possible and as much say in the decisions that affect <u>your</u> life, because I know that it will make you a better person.

CHAPTER FOURTEEN

PIP Group Module Four
- Anger -

"Anyone can become angry— that is easy; but to be angry with the right person, and to the right degree, and at the right time and for the right purpose, and in the right way— that is not easy."
— Aristotle

Part 1 - To Do Alone

Remember a time when you were angry at your child(ren)? Let yourself remember. Write down the events and what it was like for you.

_____

_____

_____

_____

_____

_____

_____

What was your Anger all about?

For example:
Was the child defiant? Refusing to do as you had told?
Did your child disobey?

Was she/he late coming home?
Were you afraid for his/her safety?
Did you feel powerless, overwhelmed?
Did you feel humiliated or shamed?
Were there family or neighbors to judge you and you felt inadequate in front of them?

Go back into yourself and search for what triggered your anger, and write down everything you can remember about your anger.

_____

_____

_____

_____

_____

_____

_____

_____

On a separate sheet of paper, write down as many significant angry times as come to your mind.

Part 2 - Your Week in Review

Part 3 - Sharing With Your PIP Group
Behind every burst of anger is a wound. Behind whatever pushes your buttons, is your own painful story. To share that story with your PIP Group, tell not only the event, but the pain associ-

ated with it: "I felt so ashamed when Johnny said that . . . I felt horrified and frightened when Kristen did . . ." "In my family, when I was a kid, we would never be allowed to talk to our parents that way!" Let your group gently hold you in their loving and caring understanding.

For those of you on the "listening crew," remember to hold all and any comments. Only reflect back with empathy and thank the person for sharing their pain.

Part 4 - Meditation

Learn to take time out for yourself. As soon as you feel anger coming, slow down, breathe in deeply, hold your breath for as long as you can and slowly exhale, releasing the tension as you let the air out.

If at all possible, remove yourself from the scene for a few minutes. Go to your own bedroom or your bathroom, or, if appropriate, you may want to walk around the block. Tell the children you are taking a 3 to 5 minute time-out and that you'll close the door because you feel angry and you don't want to explode, and you want to think through how to use your energy constructively.

Doing that is respectful of yourself and, ultimately, respectful of the children. Then, practice the following meditation:

Walking Meditation When Angry

Breathing in, I know that anger is here.
Breathing out, I know that the anger is me.
Breathing in, I know that the anger is unpleasant.
Breathing out, I know this feeling will pass.
— Thich Nhat Hanh, *Peace Is Every Step*

You might also add the following:
Breathing in, I know my anger is energy.
Breathing out, I will use my energy constructively.
— Bruce Crapuchettes

You are strong enough to take care of this anger. For the sake of your children you will <u>not</u> explode at them. Wake up every morning from now on, and make a commitment to yourself: "Today, I will be patient with the children. If I feel like exploding, I will take some time out for myself, because remaining connected with my children is my main goal, my very first priority."

"In quiet today, I tap into that powerful place inside of me that houses my anger. I allow the heat of this anger to flow through my veins and meditate on this prayer: 'The sharing of my anger is to help, not to hurt...'"

— Harville Hendrix

CHAPTER FIFTEEN

PIP Group Module Five
- Making Peace -

"When we forgive another human being, we don't erase the terrible thing he has done.... we receive him again and differently, with his flaws, with her imperfections, into the state of grace that is our wholehearted acceptance.... Forgiveness sees the wound, can remember it, is willing to work through the pain of it and, through the alchemy of forgiveness, is willing to start over."
- Daphne Rose Kingman, <u>A Garland of Love</u>

Long ago, your parents, by the very nature of being human, have caused you some hurt. It may have been slight, or maybe you are so hurt, you cannot let go of it. The pain is indelibly etched into your mind and into your memory and there, it haunts you. Thinking of all the hurt, judgment and criticism you didn't deserve, you may feel full of rage, overwhelmed and powerless.

"The only power that can stop the inexorable stream of painful memories is the 'faculty of forgiveness.' It is as simple as that."
— Hannah Arendt

Maybe it <u>is</u> "as simple as that" in principle; mostly, it is so very difficult.

For years, I held on to my hate for my mother until I realized that it was poison to me and my children. That's when I was ready to start my journey of forgiving my mother. I had to hate her fully and realize how destructive that hate was in my life before I could decide that I wanted inner peace and serenity.

That's the journey I want to invite you on today— the journey of forgiving your parents for who they were while you were growing up; grieving the parents you dreamed of but didn't get and, in all likelihood, will never have.

PART 1— To Do Alone

Grieving the parents I wished for but never had.

Mom, Dad, or _____

(fill in name of important caretaker)

I hoped you would have been: (describe your dream parents)

_____

_____

_____

_____

_____

Instead you were:

_____

_____

_____

_____

I wanted you gentle, and, sometimes, you were. At other times you were _____.

I wanted you to be patient, and, sometimes, you were. At other times, you were _____.

I wanted you to be kind, and, sometimes, you were. At other times, you were _____.

I wanted you to be understanding, and, sometimes, you were. At other times, you were _____.

I wanted you to listen to me, and, sometimes, you did. At other times, you _____.

I wanted your time and attention, and, sometimes, you gave them to me. At other times, you _____.

I wanted you to be calm, and, sometimes, you were. At other times, you were _____.

I wanted you to be proud of me, and, sometimes, you were. At other times, you were _____.

PART 2 - Your Week In Review
Same format as previously.

PART 3 - Sharing With Your PIP Group
Taking turns and mirroring each other, share with each other what your dream parents would be like; share what your real parents were like; share how it feels to you to read the paragraph in Part 4 - Meditation, below.

PART 4 - Meditation
To my imperfect parents:
Mom, Dad, I release you from being perfect, in the way I

dreamed of. I enter a journey of accepting who you were and who you are now.

You are the product of the fears and frailty of all the generations before you.

To the degree I have felt hurt by you, you, too, were feeling hurt, insecure, broken and scared. I want to be able to have compassion for your pain.

I thank you for giving me life. I begin a journey of accepting you just as you are.

This is a letter I wrote to my mother in 1995.

Dear Mom,

This year, for the first time in 28 years I called you on Mother's Day. The miracle however is not so much that I called you, but that my call wasn't motivated by guilt. It was a free, joyful giving of myself.

For years, although I may have dutifully mailed you a card, I hated Mother's Day. But it was not only Mother's Day that I hated, I hated you and I hated myself and occasionally my children. I hated the mother you had been to me, and I hated the mother I sometimes was to my children.

Our life together wasn't a pretty picture. You served me a daily diet of yelling and screaming. You ridiculed me. You shamed me in public. You broke my spirit. No words can adequately capture the intensity of my rage. I wanted to scream and scream 'til I die. Consumed by angry bitterness, I thought you embodied the essence of everything that was evil and I swore I would never forgive you, ever!

For several years, I refused to have any contact with you until you apologized. I wallowed in my pain, I nursed my bitterness and re-visited all that is horrible about you, scarring myself more and more, trapping myself deeper and deeper in a vicious circle of unrelenting hatred.

I thought I couldn't let go.

And I couldn't. I couldn't because I thought it was your responsibility to take the lead. After all you are my mother and you did cause all this pain and all this damage in me.

Over the years, I started reading and searching and struggling with my life and I learned that forgiveness wasn't something I would do for you, it is a choice I would make for myself. If I wanted to transform my life, I needed to realize that my life isn't about changing you, it's about changing me, and it's about changing the way I look at you.

Today I am beginning to realized that the abuse I suffered from you was but a reflection of the agony of your own life. But you, you were totally alone. You suffered shame and ridicule, and it is not only that you thought I was a child of the devil, but you thought you were a child of the devil. And you had no place to go - no where to turn to - no source of comfort - total loneliness - frightening disconnection.

So today, I have tears when I think of you, the little girl, so utterly lost in a cruel, inhospitable world.

I see your face, your wrinkles - what tragedy do they hide? If you could speak, what wounds would you share with me - what evil forces crushed you so violently that you were never to recover?

I don't think I will ever know, nor ever fully grasp the depth of the agony of your life.

I can only guess.

But I must never forget that my rage at you was but a shadow of your own rage. The pain you dished my way, was but a reflection of your pain.

Wayne Muller writes: "Thus family pain broke us open and set our hearts on a pilgrimage in search of love and belonging, safety and abundance, joy and peace that were missing from our childhood story. Seen through this lens, family sorrow is not only a painful wound to be endured, analyzed and treated. It may in fact become a seed that gives birth to our spiritual healing and awakening."

No where is this more true than for you and me.

So Mom, for the first time in my life, I plan to celebrate you. I am coming over there to Paris in August and am throwing a big birthday bash for you on your 80th birthday. I am finally free of my anger. I believe you have given me your best and continue to do so. You and I together make an incredible team of survivors!

Thank you, Mom.

Francine

(I never sent this letter. My mother would never understand it. I wrote it for me. But I did go and throw her a big birthday party and we all had such a great time!)

"You cannot change the past, you can only heal the hurt that comes to you from the past."
— Lewis Smedes, *The Art of Forgiving*

CHAPTER SIXTEEN

PIP Group Module Six
- Compassion For Yourself -

"It takes both the rain and the sun to make a rainbow."

The last journey I want to invite you to take is that of loving yourself.

Loving yourself means developing a sense of self-regard, a nurturing and gentle caring for the person that you are. It means learning about your unique talents. It also means that you are willing to know your shortcomings, acknowledge them, and forgive yourself.

Loving yourself is the first step toward loving your children for their sake rather than for what they can do for you. It is a lifetime commitment that requires your energy, demands lots of work, and calls you to rise above your preconceived notions. It will require integrity, compassion and all the emotional honesty you can muster.

PART 1— To Do Alone

What kind of parent did I dream of being?

When you expected your first little one, you had hopes and expectations for yourself. What were they?

_____

_____

_____

Say to yourself:

I wished I would always be kind, gentle, patient, available, understanding, selfless and sensitive. Instead, sometimes I am (write some of your negative characteristics as a parent):

_____

_____

_____

_____

_____

_____

Now say:

I acknowledge my frailties and the pain I experience around my shortcomings. I accept them as part of who I am.

I also have some wonderful qualities as a parent. (Write down your own special talents.

_____

_____

_____

_____

PART 2 - Your Week in Review

PART 3 - Sharing With Your PIP Group

Share the material in Part 1, using the format described previously of mirroring and validating each other without any extraneous comments.

The best way to learn to love yourself is to share who you are, flaws and all with your PIP Group. Listen to them mirror and validate you. Let in their caring for you. Then listen carefully to what they share and mirror accurately what they say. Work especially hard at accepting persons in your group whom you don't especially like. Learning to accept others you don't like will increase your own self love.

PART 4 - Meditation

I release myself from standards of perfection that keep me tense and anxious.

I cry for my shortcomings and revel in my strengths and talents so I can do the same for you, my precious one(s).

I accept my life as a state of grace that renews itself daily.

CHAPTER SEVENTEEN

PIP Group Module Seven
- Lean On Me, And Multiply -

"Friendships are like a spiritual garden. In the thick soil of our lives, they bloom like many beautiful flowers."

— Daphne Rose Kingman, <u>A Garland of Love</u>

I hope this is what happened to each of you over the last few months— that you have nourished each other's souls, sustained each other's spirits, and, together, blossomed magnificently. I hope that all your lives and those of your families have been enriched.

You have been kind to each other, patient with each other and respectful of one another. As a result, I trust that you are personally replenished and, therefore, better able to be available to your children.

Now is the time to decide what to do with your PIP Group. You may choose to say good-bye to one another or you may decide to continue meeting regularly. You can continue to listen to each other, validate each other's struggle and continue to practice and practice and practice again. If this experience has been helpful to you, I recommend that you buy a few of these handbooks, give them to some friends who need assistance and form another PIP Group. <u>You</u> now can become the resource person for this new group.

YOU AND YOUR CHILDREN ARE WORTH THE EFFORT!

Part Four

Bits and Pieces

CHAPTER EIGHTEEN

Two Scenarios To Practice In Your PIP Group

1. A Scenario With My Daughter

The following is an account of a conversation I recently had with my daughter. It is significant in that it was one of those conversations where I really put into practice the principles I explained in this book.

It was hard discipline on my part but well worth it. Our time on the phone together was warm, connecting, affirming, truly what I think a mother/daughter conversation ought to be like.

My daughter, who is 25 years old, finished nursing school with an AA degree and passed her State Board a year ago and received her R.N. The whole schooling process was tremendously difficult for her— she really worked very, very hard. She was not able to hold onto the first job she got. It really was too fast-paced for her. Her current job is more solid but not nearly as satisfying to her. She feels unhappy with her job. She has also decided to go for a Bachelor's in Nursing.

The other day she called and said, "Mom, do you have a minute?"
I thought, "Uh-oh, that's not like her. There must be something important coming up."
So I said, "Sure."
"Well, Mom," she said, "you know, I'm going to school right now to get my Bachelor's in nursing, but, I'm not sure that's what I want to do."
Well, so far, so good. I think I can accept that.
Then she continued, "Well, you know, I don't think that nursing is what I really want to do. I think what I would like to try is engineering."

I'm glad she was on the phone so she couldn't see my facial expression. And I really do think I was able to contain very well and stay in conversation with her.

Now in the past what I would have said would be something like, "What are you talking about? Engineering! Honey, engineering is hard! There is no way you can become an engineer! There is no way you'll be able to make it. I can't imagine you're thinking that engineering is going to be easier than nursing." Something like that.

But because I am 10 years older, because I really am committed to a different style of parenting, because I really believe that those words would have been so hurtful to my daughter and I really want to become a conscious parent, I just listened and said, "Yeah? Tell me a bit about that, Honey."

"Well, you know, Mom," she continued, "when I was in high school, I was good in math."

"Yeah, you were. That's right, I remember that."

And she went on explaining why engineering made sense to her.

"Well, you know, it certainly cannot hurt for you to try it. And it certainly seems worth it to just call some university and see what are the requirements, and what courses you have taken that could transfer. And by golly, you certainly don't have much to lose to take a semester of engineering courses and see how you take to it. Education is bound to be worth it, anyway. It seems well worth a try so you really discover for yourself."

"Yeah..."

"And especially, Honey, what I really want to tell you is I feel so much pleasure inside myself that you're not planning to stay stuck at a place that doesn't feel good to you— that you know there are choices in life and you're willing to explore those choices. That makes me feel so good that you are not going to suffer in a job that you don't like. That you are motivated and energized to say, 'Well, I am going to find a solution that works for me.' So, if there is anything that Dad and I can do to help you in gathering information for engineering or any other field, let me know."

She felt wonderful and I felt wonderful at the end of the conversation. And I knew that I was a better parent than I used to be. And it felt good.

You might say, well, aren't you leading her on? Because, as a matter of fact, my own real feeling is, wow, it's hard for me to imagine that she could get a bachelor degree in engineering. Let me tell you my thoughts about that.

First, I believe that what she was needing, seeking, yearning for was connection with me at that moment. The connection that comes from me validating who she is, validating her search, validating the idea that she came up with. I think that's my task as a parent and a big piece of learning for all of us parents. Also, in this whole interaction, she was the sender and I was just the listening parent. Not "just" because that's very hard. But I <u>was</u> the listening parent.

She wasn't asking my advice. She was sharing about herself, so it was important not to lose sight that she was telling me about <u>her</u>— her thinking, her wishes, her desire, her energies, her emotions. It was very important that I remember the conversation was <u>not</u> about me, my reactions and my thought. It was about her, sharing her journey.

Even if our children tell us that they want to have our opinion, <u>be careful</u>, be super cautious. Don't give it too quickly, maybe don't give it at all. And, if possible, refer back to them. "Well, Hon, I trust your judgment on that." Or, "I think you'll come to a decision that will be the right one for you. I have absolute trust that you will find the right decision in yourself." Because, mostly, our children are not calling us and coming to us to know our opinion as much as to share <u>theirs</u> and have their thought process honored by us and validated.

Also, who am I to think that I know better than she? I may be accurate, but what if I were not? What if indeed she did have more mathematical skills than I ever gave her credit for? Who am I to discourage her and jerk her out of her dream. What makes me think that I have been mandated to show her the light, or what I think is the light, but in fact is just my light, my reality, my thinking. I prefer to trust that she will discover for herself what works best for her. I believe it is devastating for children when parents do not have faith in them. If we don't have faith in them, how can we expect them to have faith in themselves. So, I think it's much better to let my daughter discover who she is, what she's good at, what's difficult for her. Let her teachers tell her about her limitations. Let life show her that. Let me as a parent remain connected and supportive. If she feels safe with me, if she feels connected with me and acceptable to me, she will access her true self.

Incidentally, I am happy to report that she has found a wonderful job in a hospital she loves, and she met a man there that she loves also!

Your turn:

I would like all of you to practice this same scenario in your PIP Group.

Get yourself into the place of really having doubts that your daughter— who has just finally finished college, finally passed her state boards, and is finally in a stable, professional, relatively well-paid job for the first time— makes that phone call and tells you that maybe she thinks this is the wrong path for her and that she wants to change. Can you do that?

Practice that with each other. One of you be the adult child, and another be the parent. Rotate around. Hear yourself say those words that I told my daughter.

I'm convinced that you'll benefit from that practice. If you don't practice those words at least once out loud, you probably won't be able to say them when you need to. Live practice is the best predictor of future behavior!

2. Red nail polish

A couple of weeks ago, a member of my women's group felt awful, both angry and tearful, while saying, "I really ragged at my daughter yesterday and I feel terrible about it." She told us that to soften a new rule that all the students have to now wear uniforms, her daughter's school (a private girl's school) is allowing the students to wear nail polish and earrings. Now, that was fine with her until her 13 year old daughter showed up with bright red nail polish and cheap plastic earings at which point she told us, "I just lost it."

After getting all the warmth and understanding from us, she also needed to practice the words that would have kept her connected to her daughter.

It would have sounded something like:

"I'm noticing your nail polish and your earrings. You seem very proud of them." "Yeah."

"You must feel very grown up. It's kind of nice that your school is letting you do that." "Yeah."

This is just a guess, but an educated guess based on the message communicated by her daughter. It can be a non verbal message, just a sense of pride and a "ready to conquer" look. Or it could be a verbal message such as, "Look Mom!" in an excited way.

When your child comes to you puffed with pride and pleasure, it is not the time to deflate her joy. Nothing will strengthen the bond more than your non critical acceptance of her pleasure. Although this teenage girl's taste in nail polish and jewelry was different from Mom's, she didn't do anything wrong. She was merely flapping her wings and developing her sensuous self. Mom's genuine appreciation of her pleasure is the best way to insure that Mom be one of her heroes. And children have a propensity for emulating their heroes. But Mom's judgment and criticisms were a sure way to train her daughter to cling on to red nail polish.

At a later time when they're close together emotionally, Mom could say something like, "You seem to really like red nail polish." Eventually, if her daughter feels safe because she hasn't been criticized, she will ask, "Well, what color do you like, Mom?" or "Do you like red nail polish?" Answer your truth with soft gentleness. "Oh, red is probably not my favorite color." The daughter might say, "Oh, you don't like it?" and Mom could say, "I don't like it too much on me." "Why not?" "That's a good question . . . I think it's because when I was a kid red nail polish was associated with being a loose woman." "Wow, I never thought of that . . . I like it because it's bright and I love bright colors."

You can imagine how a conversation might go if the bond between mother and daughter is not ruptured, and the daughter is not afraid of being judged or preached at. Under those conditions they can deepen their respectful partnership.

I also believe that it's Mom's best insurance against her daughter clinging on to red nail polish. In her search for power, she does not have to cling on to her red nail polish, because there is no injunction against it. She does not have to gain control of her life through defying Mom's distaste for red nail polish, because Mom didn't try to control her life.

If parents are willing to focus on becoming friends, rather than controlling their children's life, they remove the cause for rebellion and pave the parenting journey with good will.

Now, you practice this same scenario with your PIP Group.

Further work with your PIP Group

The following issues often trigger parents:
- Noise: crying, screaming, or certain type of music

- Level of activity: running, climbing, touching, breaking

- Children's need for attention

- Soiling: Toileting accidents can become a serious source of aggravation for parents.

- Grooming and appearance: make up, clothing

- Disobedience and such words as "no" "why?" "mine" "I don't want to"

You may have a low tolerance level for any of the above. Without judgement for yourself, talk to members of your PIP Group regarding those behaviors in your children that may arouse anger and discomfort in you.

Let yourself remember how your parents were with you on these topics. Also, make sure you talk to each other about your possible issue with shame or guilt. Many parents tend to do poor parenting because they let their feelings of shame or guilt make the decision for them. Children are quick to pick up on their parent's guilt and you would be prey to their manipulating you through guilt as you would be prone to do the same with them.

Make generous use of the richness and generosity of spirit between you. You need each other's understanding and support.

CHAPTER NINETEEN

The Pitfalls Of Praise

Parents are often surprised to hear me say that complimenting their children can be harmful. In fact, parents often tell me, "How can she feel I didn't support her and did not appreciate her? I gave her lots of compliments all the time!" The problem with compliments is that they are often experienced by the child as pressure to perform.

If a parent tells a child, "Wow, honey, you're so good at drawing. You're such a great artist!" The child will experience that as a compliment only if he feels good about his drawing. In this case, the remark is an accurate reflection of how the child feels, and will therefore be received as a compliment— just the way it was intended to be.

If, on the other hand, the child feels discouraged and unsatisfied with the way his drawing turned out, your compliment will only bring discomfort and disconnection. Your "you're so good" only brings a "no, I'm not." It is best to find out how your child feels first before you make a compliment. Then you can say something like, "Your teacher gave you an A, but you don't feel good about it." — or, "You seem discouraged with your project even though you got a good grade." This is how to stay on the mirroring path.

Also, when your child brings a drawing home, rather than say, "You're such a good little artist," make some neutral comment such as, "I like the way you put the orange and yellow next to each other like that," and, "I'm wondering if that's our house?"

If you keep your comments neutral, you will remain safe, and the children will feel free to share more with you because there are no judgments, negative or positive, attached to your comments.

Judgments are always painful, even positive judgments. They create a lack of safety and disruption in the relationship.

I was reading a parent manual recently, and, as is often the case, I felt disturbed by the kind of advice that is printed for parents. One suggestion was to say, "I'm proud of you." The problem I have with "I'm proud of you" is that it's patronizing of the child. The assumption is, "I'm proud of you because I really didn't believe you could do it and since you did do it, I am proud of you." Evaluate the following: Would we say those words to someone we consider equal or superior to us? Would we say those words to our supervisor or our boss? Probably not. Those words, "I am proud of you" imply a hierarchy, a ladder. It implies that I know better than you. I am above you. And because I know better than you and I am above you, I can evaluate what you've done; and therefore, that's why I feel proud of you. I give my seal of approval to what you've said or what you've done.

I believe that this way of thinking moves us out of the partnership concept and into the autocratic, hierarchical dimension. It is potentially a dangerous phrase that could convey something negative to the child. I would rather replace it with, "You seem to be proud of yourself. You've worked hard. It's fun to see how hard you've tried and I really feel happy for you."

We must learn to mirror the intensity of their pleasure, as well. We must raise our voice and be excited with them at a level that matches their excitement in order to be an accurate mirror.

Stay on a reflective path with your child !

Another piece of advice in that manual was to tell the child, "I couldn't have done it without you." If that is absolutely true and, in fact, you could not have done it without the child, then, by all means, say, "Honey, thank you, I could not have done it without you. I'm so appreciative." Those are wonderful words.

Sometimes, though, I am afraid those words would be used in the same patronizing tone as "I'm proud of you"— trying to make the child feel good and saying, "I couldn't have done it without you" as if that was going to help the child feel better about herself. But, in fact, unless it is the absolute truth that "I couldn't have done it without you", it will make the child feel bad. The child will know that it lacks integrity and if it lacks integrity, then it's done to placate the child and it's likely to backfire on you. It would be a dangerous path to take.

Another piece of advice was to say, "Good job!" Again, I think those words are potentially dangerous because maybe the child feels he or she did not do a good job, in which case, once again, better mirror.

"It looks like you feel really good about your job."
"Yeah!"
"You really have done well, haven't you?"
"Yeah."
"You seem to be really proud of all this hard work you've put into it."
"Yeah."
"Well, that certainly makes sense to me. I saw all the hard work you put into it. Thank you, Honey."

Sometimes the parent says "Good job" because they think that's going to be encouraging; in fact, the child may feel crummy about the work, the child may not like what he or she has written, the child may not like the grade or the report card. Saying "Good job" is not being sensitive to the child's emotion about that.

Once again, to really be a sensitive, collaborative parent in partnership with your child, put yourself in the mode of reflecting back what the child is trying to convey to you. If your child seems pleased, say "You seem pleased with your work! I have noticed all your efforts. I am happy for you!" If your child seems unhappy or disappointed, reflect that:

"I like your painting but you seem disappointed with it."
"Yeah, it's crummy."
"You don't like the way it turned out."

This puts you both in a place of integrity and strengthens the connection.

As parents, before we speak, let's listen to what our children are feeling first because then and only then can we reflect back with accuracy and hopefully warmth, caring, and gentleness.

CHAPTER TWENTY

Bedtime

This is a very real concern for many parents.

If your child is three and older, deal with the situation during your Family Round Table. Make every effort to understand your child's concerns and fears. Empathize with her by saying, "It's really scary at night. Are there monsters under the bed?"

Let him know you understand, not with the words, "I understand," but with such words as, "It's more fun to stay up with the grown ups. You don't want to miss on all the fun." Say whatever your child is telling you. Be sensitive to your children. Learn to become attuned to their needs. Master the art of picking up what they are trying to tell you.

If you are dealing with young infants, rest assured that you cannot spoil them. Every cry is a cry for help. Let yourself feel the terror of the very young and make yourself available again and again. Your sacrifice now is the building block of a secure foundation. It will pay off many times over when your child is older.

You may have been given the advice to ignore your infant's crying at night and especially not to pick them up. They will probably fall asleep out of sheer exhaustion. This is known as "Ferberizing a child"— a term coming from the man who originally made this recommendation. In my opinion, this is an awful and cruel experience repeated thousands of times every night across America.

Sadly, this is what I did with my children 30 years ago. I feel deep pain about it. I now see it as true child abuse. How can I have closed my heart to their needs in such a way? I did it because I wanted "to do it right!"

But what is right is to follow your natural instinct of tender loving for this little person entrusted to your care. Interpret every cry as, "I need you right now. I am afraid. I need the comfort of your presence— the warmth of your body— the caress of your hand— the taste of your milk."

If the infant's cry is met with coldness and rejection, it will learn that the world is not a safe place. These little ones will learn that they are not welcome, and in order not to feel their pain, they will begin to block off their emotions and become "tough." This experience, repeated too many times during their young formative years, is what a killer is made up of.

So instead, consider the family bed alternative. Have your infants sleep with you. That is what has been done for eons of time, and that is what your child's brain has been designed to do. You will all sleep better. Reserve the notion of his bed and his room for a later time when he is older. You can let her sleep on the floor by your bed for a long time.

When your children are ready to have their own bed or their own room, they will let you know. Remember, they are genetically programmed to seek independence. Unless you interfere negatively with their nature, it will all happen in its own time. Follow their leadership. They know when they are ready.

For more on this topic, read Robert Wright, *The Moral Animal: Evolutionary Psychology and Everyday Life.* Also, read the 20th anniversary special edition of the magazine called, *Mothering*, No 81, Winter, 1996.

More bedtime thoughts

At a later age, it is the power struggle that you let yourself get into with your child that fuels the desire in the child to not go to bed and not give into his tiredness. You want to avoid the power struggle at all costs. Flow with them as much as possible. If the child discovers that bedtime is extremely important to you, a power struggle over it will show him the way to have power over you, or will show her how to be a little tyrant. But if you let go of controlling bedtime and you can flow with them as much as possible, then their natural tiredness will carry them through. Once again, you have to learn to really have faith in them.

A bedtime suggestion:

When you tuck them in for the night, ask your children, "What was the best thing that happened to you today?" And, "What was the worst thing that happened to you today?"

Share with them also by saying, "Well, the best thing that happened to me today was . . . " And then say, "The worst thing that happened to me today was . . . " And tell them about your day. If they hear a ring of honesty, they will want to share their day with you.

CHAPTER TWENTY ONE

Sibling Rivalry

Maybe your experience is, "Individually, the kids are great. It's when they are together that they make me a nervous wreck because of their constant bickering at each other, teasing, and otherwise obnoxious behavior which they seem to reserve for each other."

"Mom, he hit me," followed by, "She stole my truck," "No, I didn't", "Yes you did", and so on— all in a whiny, high-pitched tone guaranteed to put you off kilter despite your best intentions.

Before we move to solutions, let me tell you about sibling rivalry.

Human beings are driven by the urge to survive. Children are no different and they intuitively know that in order to stay alive, they must remain connected to their parents at all cost. It is easy for children to feel insecure and to worry about their connection to Mom and Dad. So they've got to frequently check out that they're important to you, at least as important as their brother or sister— hopefully, more! They could simply ask, "Mom (Dad), am I still important to you? I want to make sure you haven't forgotten me." Unfortunately, they do not have the capacity to think that clearly, much less verbalize such complicated thoughts. And besides, there is a much easier way to get the same result! They can quarrel with their sibling, thus ensuring they'll get your attention. I would dare bet that it works every time. And if it doesn't, they'll up the ante until it does work.

Sibling rivalry is genetically programmed to ensure the child's survival and is, therefore, a normal aspect of your child's psycho-logical makeup. Hopefully, knowing that will help you relax. You haven't given birth to a set of monsters, but to healthy children who desperately need to feel connected with you. And they need lots and lots of attention— yours. And they need reassurance that they are important to you.

Each child wants to pull you on his or her side and cast a shadow on the other child, seeking to elevate him or herself at the expense of the other.
There is a great, great temptation for you to interfere, based on what you have observed. But getting involved in your children's quarrels is a trap. As soon as you take a stance, you have "gotten hooked" and have lost the battle.

Your best bet is to learn to stay out of your children's quarrels because the minute you do get involved, they win and have power over you. In addition, even though you may think you saw the whole event, children have such subtle ways to provoke one another, ways that you most likely have missed.

So, what do you do?

Resist the temptation to know what happened and to take sides. Sometimes the provocation may have been a look, a tongue sticking out, or any movement which you couldn't have heard and probably didn't see (your children are smart— trust me).

So, you would say something like the following:

"The two of you (or however many there are) seem to be having a problem right now. I'm sure you can find a solution. I'll close the door to the kitchen to keep my peace and quiet while you work it out."

And you do just that— detach emotionally from the children's squabbling.

or,

if it gets to you too much, tell them, "Your quarreling is disturbing to me. I'm going to my bedroom— my bathroom— for the next five minutes."

or,

you could say, "It looks like the two of you have a problem to put on the agenda for our next Family Round Table."

When one child comes to you saying, "He did that," or "She said that," reply by saying, "Mary, it looks like you have something to tell Nathan." After Mary tells her complaint directly to the person who is the cause of her distress, rather than you, an innocent bystander, ask Nathan, "Nathan, do you have anything you would like to tell Mary?"

I also strongly suggest that you teach your children to mirror each other. Not to mirror you, you are the adult, but their peers, their siblings, and classmates. It is good training to really learn to listen and learn to incorporate somebody else's divergent opinion.

You will discover that if you refuse to get involved in your children's squabbles, they have the inner resources to solve their problems. If you refuse to involve yourself in their affairs, they will lose a great deal of incentive to quarrel in the first place.

"What if one child gets hurt?" you might ask. I would still stick to the plan of detachment and non-involvement and let them sort out their problems. Let the hurt child take initiative to solve his or her problem. If you intervene, you inadvertently disempower the child. If you come to the rescue (short of a life-threatening situation which would be extremely rare), you have conveyed the message, "I don't think you are strong enough or smart enough to look after yourself, and solve your own problems." From the children's perspective it will look like you have taken sides in favor of the hurt child and against the other(s).

If you happen to be on a road, pull to the side (get off the Freeway if necessary) and tell them: "I am finding it difficult to drive well and concentrate when you guys are quarreling. I'll wait until you come to an agreement." Lean your seat back, close your eyes, and wait it out.

If you can't wait because of a <u>true</u> deadline, make sure you bring up the problem at the Family Round Table and ask the children what would be helpful to them and what solution they suggest, especially agreeing ahead of time on what will happen if they quarrel in the car.

Make sure that you do not agree to put yourself in the situation of judging who is right and who is wrong or who started and who continued. Keep on an absolutely neutral course— kind, warm, understanding AND neutral.

Your gentle but firm refusal to participate in their power struggle or to try to reason with them or cajole them will pay off. In time they will learn to solve their own problems.

CHAPTER TWENTY TWO

Setting Your Boundaries

1. Candy

Cathy Guisewite, in her comic strip called *Cathy,* always seems to capture human dilemmas so wonderfully. Recently, she spoke to an endemic parent problem: "Shall I let her do that, or shall I not?"

Is it okay for her to eat one more candy or is she supposed to wait 'til after dinner? The mother's own reflections read: "Who knows? There are a hundred events a day where I know I'm supposed to draw a line, but I have no idea where the line's supposed to be! Even worse, I have to stand by the line I've drawn knowing full well it was based on nothing but a frantic arbitrary attempt to appear to be in charge!!"

Does all that sound familiar?

The answer is as follows: First, do read and educate yourself as much as you can. There's a plethora of parenting material available. Read and make a decision that makes sense to you. Second, keep to the following guidelines: Am I preserving the bond with my child? and— Am I relating in a way that validates the desire and does not induce shame or guilt on the child?

Then remain firm in your decision. If you discover later that you made the wrong decision, then simply acknowledge it. You're not supposed to know what you don't know. But stay kind yet firm on whatever makes sense to you for the moment.

You see, regardless of where you draw the line, your child, if s/he is a normal child will want to test you to see if you really mean it. Learn to mean what you say. Often I tell clients, "Own your decision!"

If your child wants a candy and you want to say no, say: "Boy, I can imagine that a (another) candy would taste really good. It's getting close to supper time and I would rather not." Remain calm and firm. When the child asks again, don't be irritated. The child has the right to ask again. Repeat the same answer.

Your life would be a lot easier if your children didn't push you, but your children are not here to protect you against your own weaknesses. They're here to promote your growth!

It is not helpful to say, "How many times do I have to tell you?" or, "I told you before!"

If their asking is getting to you, tell them! "Honey, I feel anxious when you keep asking. I'd like to ask you to stop asking for more candy (or money)." You may want to give them the reason, in which case, give them the real reason. For example, say, "I do have some money which I am keeping for paying the bills. So, I don't want to give you any money right now." Rather than, "I don't have any money," when in fact our children know full well you do have some money. It may feel like a white lie to you. But, in fact, when you do that you are teaching them to be dishonest.

It is hard to say no because we fear to be seen as the "bad guy" or the "heavy." This is why it is important that you fully believe in your innocence and your goodness.

Sometimes it is so hard to say no that it becomes easier if you yell or become sharp in some way. But that hurts the child. You must learn to say no in a warm, gentle, and caring manner. Say no with compassion. Practice with your PIP Group. That's what the members of your group are for.

If you do not give yourself permission to say no, you will not give your children permission to say no when they feel like saying no. It will hurt your relationship. If you can allow yourself to say no truthfully, then your yes will also be more real and more meaningful. It will not be a capitulation just because no is so hard to say.

2. Stay in another room

I was with friends recently who just adopted a 7 year old boy. And of course they want to be supportive of him and really convey their love for him and their desire to have him in their lives. All of which makes absolute sense to me.

But that evening was an evening for adults. We had spent time with the child and had taken him to McDonald's where he had great fun playing with some of the play equipment that was there, which was wonderful. And time was taken with him with great warmth and caring and gentleness and just a wonderful parenting job. And when 8 o'clock came, it was time for the adults to spend some time together. It was so difficult for those parents to convey that to the little boy. And, of course, the little boy was not particularly wanting to cooperate and have to give up the spotlight.

My recommendation there would be to say the words, "McDonald's was a lot of fun and I've really enjoyed the time we've had. Now I want to spend some time with Francine. So, Honey, this is the choice that I want to give you. You can be in the room here with us. I would love that, if you want to. But you would have to remain quiet. When you feel like talking or moving or playing— which is perfectly fine with me— what I would like you to do is go into the next room, in the dining room, and then we'll still see you. We'll sort of be together but there you can write and you can play and you can do what you want. Or another choice is you can go into your room upstairs. In this room here for the next couple of hours, we're just going to be doing adult things. Which would you like to do?

Put the responsibility on the child. Let the child make a choice.

What those parents actually did is that they started quite well but then when the child became very disruptive they started making mistakes— we were watching a video about adoption, it was a wonderful video— they allowed the child to violate their boundaries over and over and over again. It's so difficult to honor our own boundaries. It feels in your guts as if honoring your own boundaries means that you are mean, that you are a bad parent, that maybe you are harsh. But it really doesn't mean any of that. It is not harsh unless you use a harsh tone of voice, or harsh words.

But if you just stop and say, "Right now, Honey, I'm really feeling disrupted and I'd like you to make a choice. You can stay in this room but you have to be quiet. You can be on my lap and I'd love that. Or you can go in another room and play. Which would you like to do? Would you like to be in this room and be quiet or would you like to be in another room so you can play?"

And stop everything until the child makes a decision. And if the child makes no decision then you have to make a decision for the child. And say, "Right now I am busy and I am wanting to watch this video and so I am going to put you into the other room." And then bring that up at the next Family Round Table. "I have a frustration: I have a problem when I am busy at night and you make noise and I feel disrupted." Put your heads together during the Family Round Table trying to generate solutions to that problem. Make sure you involve the child in the solution.

You might do that even that night. "This is my proposal: You can either be in this room and in this room you would have to be quiet. Or you can be in the next room and you can draw and paint and play. Or, you can go up to your room and maybe read. Or, maybe you have your own idea." And see if the child can generate an idea that would be acceptable to you.

What you want to avoid is to say the words, "This is going to be a time where I am not going to pay attention to you. I am actually going to be doing an adult thing with my friends" and then you let the child interrupt the process over and over and over again. Then your words lack integrity. Also, you run the risk of reaching the end of your rope and exploding at the child. And that, of course, would be the worst case scenario.

You want to remain grounded and you want to remain strong, calm, warm, accepting, and respecting your own boundaries. If you don't learn to do that, then your children will never learn to respect their boundaries because you yourself as parents do not know how to respect your own boundaries.

I'd like you to practice in your PIP Group when there is a child that is interruptive and disruptive for you to say something like the following:

"Honey,"(or the name of the child— maybe we'll call this child Eric) "You can stay in this room. I can see that it's really difficult when Mommy and Daddy are busy and I'm not paying attention to you. That makes sense that it's not fun for you. Yeah, I can imagine that you would like me to pay attention to you and drop everything I'm doing. That really makes sense to me. Right now, for the next two hours, that's not what I want to do. I want to spend time with Dad, watching this video. And so, Eric, what would you like to do? You can stay here and sit quietly on my lap. You can be in this room but in order to be in this room, you'll have to be quiet. Or, you can go into the next room and still see us and you can draw and paint and play with your games. Or, you can go upstairs in your bedroom if you wish. Which would you like to do, or do you have any other ideas?"

Stay with your position even to the point of having to ask the child to stay in the next room. And then again, bring that up at the Family Round Table if there is a problem.

It will take time for your children to learn that you are expecting them to respect your boundaries. That's mostly because in the past you haven't required them to do so. You say you want them to respect your boundaries and you threaten. Then you probably do not act upon the threats.

Stop the threats. Remain firm, warm, kind, and stick to your boundaries.

3. Mommy, do you still love me?

A client of mine which I will call Kirsten, was sharing the following with me. Because her husband had just left them, she let her eight year old daughter Jessica sleep in bed with her. One week day night, she went into her bedroom around ten to find her daughter watching TV, munching on popcorn and gingerly patting the bed indicating to her Mom non verbally, "Come and join me Mom. Let's watch and munch together."

Mom's blood churned. Her words flew out of her mouth before she had a chance to think. She turned off the TV, told her daughter off, and slammed the bedroom door behind her as she retreated into the hallway. She thought to herself, "You allow your child to sleep in your bed and that's what you get in return."

Her daughter's sobbing disturbed her. She thought for a moment, "What would Francine tell me. Oh, yes. Keep the connection alive. That's always the first step."

She took a deep breath and went back into the bedroom, "you were looking forward to having fun with me . . . and you had prepared a special surprise, and you were hoping I'd sit and watch TV with you?" Jessica nodded her head. "And then I came in was angry and yelled at you." Jessica sniffled as her sobbing began to subside. "That must have been so disappointing to you honey." "Yeah."

"Tell you what. Because it is a school night it is important to me that you turn off the lights at 9 pm. But tomorrow is Friday and I'd love to sit down, watch TV, and eat popcorn together. Would that be okay?" Jessica had a big smile. Mom turned the lights off and just as she was about to leave the room, Jessica asked, "Mommy, do you still love me?"

Mom: "I guess it is hard for you to know that I love you when I get angry at you like that. That makes sense to me. I love you so much, honey. You are so precious to me."

I love this story, partly because it is a true story, but also because this mother really understood how to be firm and compassionate at the same time. She honored her boundaries (9 pm bedtime was important to her) while still learning to respect her daughter and stay connected with her. It also shows us that when we make mistakes, and we will, it can always be recovered. Nothing is ever lost forever.

4. I want that toy!

You take your three year old grocery shopping with you and within minutes, he has spotted a coveted toy. He starts crying and behaves in a way that is generally embarrassing to you. What do you say or do?

The first step is to be reflective of his emotional state while remaining warm and connecting. "That really looks good . . . You would like Mommy to buy that for you . . . I can see that, Stevie. It makes sense to me that it would be fun to have that . . . (pause) I do not want to buy you a toy right now."

Don't explain why. That only gives away the fact that you are feeling insecure about your decision. Notice that I am not recommending to say, "I can't buy you this right now." Chances are that you could. You simply don't want to. That is your perfect right.

Own that decision as yours. When you say you can't, you disempower yourself.

Stevie: "Why?" . . . more crying.

Mom: "You hate it when Mommy says no. You really would like Mommy to say yes. . . . (pause) I have decided not to buy toys when we go to the grocery store."

Another, "Why? . . .

Mom: "Why? . . . Because I feel uncomfortable buying you toys whenever we go grocery shopping together." Here, do not add the words, "That's why." Those last two words could feel cutting and matter of fact. But remember you want to set your boundaries through your actions, not through threatening words or a curt tone of voice.

Remain kind, calm, warm, and stay firm in the boundaries you have set.

If your child continues to cry in a manner that you feel is disruptive to other customers, tell your child, "I'm having a hard time with your crying and I want to go to the car for a few minutes." Ask the cashier to watch your cart and go to your car with your child to re-center yourself.

Remember, stay away from any teachy/preachy urge you may have. You have probably tried the teachy/preachy admonition route in the past. Probably without much success. That is because children are not well suited to respond to angry words. With regards to disciplining your children, the fewer the words the better.

When you get home, don't forget to write your frustration on the agenda for your next Family Round Table. At that time (no, not before) ask your child if there is something you could do to help him accept that you will not buy him a toy or candy when the two of you go grocery shopping.

You may want to consider going grocery shopping without your child. And if you do not have a partner at home, you may exchange service with one of your PIP Group members.

Do not blame or shame your child for trying to twist your arm. He is doing the "right" thing, namely, testing the limits . . . checking on your word. If you can gently but firmly stick to your words, he will develop a sense of trust in you and that will help you develop a secure child.

CHAPTER TWENTY THREE

Loving Our Children

In my practice, I have not encountered a parent who did not love their children, or at least believed they loved their children. They all had good intentions and wanted the best for them.

In my search to understand what love means, I have run across the following ideas: The essence of love is not to use the other to make us happy, but to serve and uphold the one we love. Love wants to affirm rather than judge. Love doesn't impose impossible standards, but appreciates and honors "that which is" even if "that which is" is humble and down to earth.

Understood this way, few of us know how to love, because few of us have been loved.

Most of us have to make profound changes in ourselves in order to move past our egos and learn to really love our children for who they are. We need to learn to love our children rather than the projections we impose on them, or the expectations that they fulfill <u>our</u> dreams.

Our love, then, would affirm the person they actually are— slow, messy, loud, rambunctious, or homely. Our love for our children would cause us to value them as total selves, the bad and the good, the negative and the positive, when they don't agree with us as well as when they do. Our love would appreciate fully their intrinsic value and respectfully uphold their importance.

Loving our children will transform us

and the world we live in!

Part Five

Conscious and
Unconscious
Parenting

CHAPTER TWENTY FOUR

Twelve Indicators Of Unconscious Parenting *

When we have a hard time listening to our children, when we punish them to "teach them a lesson," when we use words like "I know" and "but" or any of those words on "The Wall" (see p. 47), we are not bad people. In fact, all the parents I have worked with are good people wanting the best for their children. At the same time, however, I believe they are mistaken, and the word I like to use is that they are "unconscious" in their parenting. Most of us are unconscious in the way we parent our children. I certainly was unconscious when my children were younger and I find that to be true for the many parents I work with. I want to clarify what I mean by "unconscious parenting."

The following are what I call "The Twelve Indicators Of Unconscious Parenting."

1. The first indicator of unconscious parenting is when we believe that punishing our children will make them good even though it hasn't worked. We have punished, spanked, shamed, and humiliated our children. We have made them feel guilty, put them in time-out, and bribed them over and over and we are worse off today than ever before. In our "enlightenment" we have shifted from using punishment to using "behavior modification" in our schools and in our homes for many years now. We use time-out when they are bad, and happy faces, gold stars, and compliments when they are good. Quite sadly, I have to say that for a period of time we raised our own children on a token economy model and to this day, our 27 year old son is still angry at the way we tried to

---

* I am indebted in this chapter to Harville Hendrix for the idea that we all live life unconsciously. He gave an inspiring plenary address at the national conference of the Association For Imago Relationship Therapy in Chicago in 1993, where he presented "The Ten Indicators of Unconsciousness." He was speaking of people in general. Here I am applying the "we live unconsciously" idea to parenting. Five of mine are very similar to his and I certainly want to give him credit.

144

manipulate him. He would have a lot to tell you of his experience as a child with red, white, and blue chips and charts covering the hallway. Behavior modification (or any form of rewards and punishment) only gives temporary relief. It didn't work for me, because it just does not work! If it did, we wouldn't have to do it so often. But we continue to do it and many specialists in child-hood development still recommend it even though research and our personal experience has taught us that it doesn't work.

We try to convince our children and ourselves that punishments are something they deserve and we delude ourselves into thinking that "it will teach them a lesson." We think, "They have to pay the consequenses of their actions." I am reminded of this quote:

> *"Punishing children does not make them good,*
> *just as punishing ourselves does not make us good.*
> *It is the belief that we need to be punished that*
> *prevents us from seeing that we are already good."*

- Cheri Huber and Melinda Guyol (see appendix)

2. The second indicator of unconscious parenting is when we blame our children. One way we do this is to tell them, "You make me . . . " "You make me sick." "You make me tired." "You're driving me nuts." We say these words without taking any sense of personal responsibility. We don't even blink an eye. "You make me nervous." "You make me angry." We really believe our children are responsible for our state of being. What a cruel paradox this is. We are supposed to model for them what personal responsibility means! "If you hadn't been so impatient, I wouldn't have gotten into this accident."
"If you were more considerate, I wouldn't be so tired."

3. The third indicator of a lack of consciousness is when we make excuses, something we do generously with our children. We might say something like, "Well, honey, you're taking it the wrong way." (There's a little blaming there.) Or, "I didn't mean it that way." "If you only knew how busy I have been . . . " Let's assume that we had promised our children to take them out for some outing on Saturday and when something happens that prevented us from making good on our promise, and the children show some form of disappointment or maybe even anger that things are not going to happen the way we said it would, we usually go on explaining why it is the way it is. "Well, this happened and that happened and it's out of my control and there is nothing I can do about it and you're going to have to take it because that's the way it is!" It is another indication of our lack of consciousness when we go on giving explanations and excuses, because then we are focusing on exonerating ourselves rather than empathizing with the children's disappointment.

4. The fourth indicator of unconsciousness is when we describe the character and the motivation of our children to them or to other adults, especially in front of them. We tend to interpret our children's behavior. "Oh, you're being impossible. You're out of control. You're not being cooperative. You're trying to get to me. You're trying to manipulate me." And sometimes we do that with positive behaviors as well. We might say, "You're being so good." or "You're much better at math than Johnny is." And sometimes we explain our children to our friends. Just imagine for a moment. A mother meets another mother at the mall or at the grocery store and they go on jabbering about their respective children. "He's doing so well at school, and we just got our report back and the teacher says this, and that, and she is just the best in her gymnastics class." We talk about our children to other adults in front of them as if they did not exist. That is profoundly disrespectful of the child. Symbolically, it is as if the child did not exist and it becomes an annihilation of the person of the child. If the comments are positive and we make these positive interpretations and comments about the child in front of the child, it becomes terribly embarrassing for the child. If the comments are negative, it is humiliating. We often indulge into that kind of behavior and when we do, that's another indicator that we are unconscious parents.

5. The fifth indicator of unconscious parenting is to believe that our children experience things the way we do. Consider how easy it is for us to say, "Oh, it can't hurt that badly." "Don't you love this book?" or, "I like Mrs. Smith, I think she is a fabulous teacher, don't you?" And if our children say no, we feel shocked!

Another classic example would be when our child protests bedtime, you say, "Darling, it's already 10 o'clock!"— implying that at such a late hour you have to be tired! Trapped in our lack of consciousness, we cannot validate that our child is experiencing the moment very differently than we are.

6. **The sixth indicator of unconscious parenting is when we devalue our children when their opinion is different than ours.** Sometimes we might do it with straight words, such as, "That's a stupid idea, that's just crazy thinking, honey." But often times we're not quite that direct. Instead, we convey it with our attitude, our inflection, our tone of voice. A tone that means, "You dummy." Though we may not use these words, they are implied, especially when combined with sarcasm. "Do you really think you're going to get anywhere with these kinds of grades?" "Can't you see that those two don't match?" "Couldn't you have figured it out by yourself?" "The Jones are not worth spending time with and I can't believe you're friends with Johnny."

Without using the words specifically, we still convey to our children: "That's ridiculous!" "That's stupid." "You don't make any sense." They are quick to translate that into their mind as, "I am stupid!" and, "I am ridiculous!"— and they end up believing there is something wrong with them.

7. The seventh indicator of unconscious parenting is to

believe that we live in the present. Your child comes in the house with a large grin on her dirty face, messy hair, ruffled dress, and your blood curdles. You lash out at her. Her messiness distresses you. Yet , after you are able to look at the situation rationally, no real damage has been done— nothing that a shower and a washing machine cannot fix. Still you feel triggered. Your reaction is very real.

What is probably happening is that you have internalized your parents' views on cleanliness. You know, "Cleanliness is next to Godliness!" and when your daughter comes home looking dirty, you suddenly feel as if you are a "bad" mother. You know that is what your mother would think if she were here. And you know what? She is here! She is internalized inside your brain. You are not just responding to the current situation, you are reacting to your past and your own history.

We project our unfinished business, our unfulfilled desires, and our unresolved pain onto our children. I certainly did that. I wanted my children to have piano lessons. That was very impor- tant to me when they were growing up. But the main reason was not that they were particularly interested, but that I had always wanted to take piano lessons and I didn't get a chance to. So it became very important to me that my children had something that I didn't have. For the same reason, I dragged them to many con- certs, ballets, and plays. Our decisions as parents are often based on what we either got that we didn't want as a child, or didn't get but did want. In either one of those situations, we're trapped into unconscious parenting. If a parent says, "I am doing this because my parents never did that for me," then the decision and the behavior of the parent is grounded into their own childhood rather than grounded in an attunement to the child's current needs. Therefore it is indicative of unconscious parenting.

8. The eighth indicator of unconscious parenting is to believe that children are undeserving of respect simply because

148

they are children. This goes with the corollary that we parents deserve respect just because we are parents. It is a sad state of affairs that we often think that because our children are children, they can be treated with disrespect. We parents do deserve respect because we are parents, and also, children deserve respect because they are children. All of us deserve respect because we are human beings. And we deserve respect not because of our position in life but because of our existence as living, breathing human beings. It is our very existence that demands respect.

9. The ninth indicator of unconscious parenting is when we believe that we know our children better than they know themselves. Now, to be certain, we know more about math and how to read and write or how to get from here to there. That's part of our life experience and learning. But because of this, sometimes we are easily lulled into believing that we also know our children's internal reality better than they know their own internal reality. Of course, that's what gives us permission to interpret them the way we do. Because of this we tend to impose our reality onto them without a lot of concern about their own reality, about their own subjective experience. The truth is that often their subjective realities, their needs, are an inconvenience to us, so we don't want to know them. We want to impose our, more convenient to us, view of the world. And when we do that, we're trapped into unconscious parenting.

World peace can only begin when we start to believe and truly integrate into the fabric of our thinking that children have just as much to contribute to our development as parents as we do to their development as children. We need to believe that our children are our spiritual equals and to learn to honor and respect their spiritual contribution to our lives!

10. The tenth indicator of unconscious parenting is to believe that children must learn obedience to develop self-discipline. Most of us force our children to be obedient. That is certainly what I did to my children when they were young and that is what happened to me when I was young. Therefore, as the good unconscious parent that I was, I did to my children what was done to me, that is, <u>demand</u> obedience from my children, which can always be accomplished through threats and manipulation. As long as we are the adults and have the power, we can always force obedience and "break their will." That is, until they become teenagers. What happens when we do this is that children develop an internalized desire for vengeance that will eventually be played out. The anger can be played out against society and the child might slip into anti-social behavior. The development of gangs is an example of that in our society today. Also, the anger caused by dictatorial parenting can be turned inward and promote feelings of despair and isolation leading to suicide. The rate of teenage suicide is on the rise, and sadly enough, that's probably because as unconscious parents, we have been trapped into believing that forced obedience develops self-discipline in our children.

Self-discipline, by definition, needs to come from the Self (I capitalize the word Self because it is so sacred). To the degree that we autocratically dictate from the outside, then the discipline is outside the Self and it is no longer Self-discipline, but discipline based on others: either the fear of others or the desire to please others. This is the opposite of the discipline that springs from inside the Self.

11. The eleventh indicator of unconscious parenting is when we believe that a child's pretense of gratitude or sorrow is better than the real feelings, or, that a feeling of duty produces love. We force them to say things that are important for us but may not be true for them, for example, "Tell her you're sorry!" The reason we do that is because we are good people trying to do the right thing. We think that forcing them to say something that is not true for them is going to train them to be honest, giving, generous, kind, and good citizens. But in fact, all we're doing is training them to lie, training them to disconnect with their true feelings, and training them to believe that the way they behave is more important than the way they are. They learn that it is worth sacrificing the Self in order to be acceptable. This sets up the groundwork for becoming split as adults, because as children they were experiencing one thing but we demanded that they say or do something else.

12. The twelfth indicator of unconscious parenting is to believe that children are to be seen and not heard. This is deeply ingrained in our society. I was raised in France, and French children were to remain quiet at the dinner table. Never speak unless spoken to. This is not as strict a rule in America (most families don't eat together any more anyway), but I have observed this belief present here consistently also. This is the world upside down and it shows the depth of our lack of consciousness. Children ought to be heard and ought to be heard first! And if they feel heard, they will also experience themselves as being seen and having intrinsic worth.

Looking at these indices of unconscious parenting, they cluster around two main ideas. The first idea centers on our tendency to feel guilty and badly about who we are as a result of the way we were parented. We do not want to be held responsible when something negative happens. That would confirm that we are guilty and therefore bad. What we do instead is to make our children accountable for the negative in our lives. Because of our perceived "non-goodness," we either blame our children and put the responsibility on them, or we spend endless hours explaining ourselves to them. We tell them why we did or didn't do this or that, wanting them to know of our goodness, which we are doubting in the first place. We burden them with the job of proving us innocent.

The second cluster is around our terror of being relative and unimportant. To the degree that we feel unimportant, we feel disempowered as well. Steeped in our lack of consciousness, we compensate by being autocratic and dictatorial with our children. We repeatedly put ourselves at the center of our children's universe. This gives us an illusion of power. The greater the gap between our need to be absolute and our perceived powerlessness, the greater our need to apply an authoritarian style of parenting.

Because of our terror to be found "bad," we seek absolution and redemption through our children. Because of our terror to be relative and not absolute, we experience an urge to dictate how things will be and we have a deep drive to control our children and to stick ourselves in the middle of what they want to do or say. We want to run the show and overshadow the child.

If we go back and look at the twelve indices of unconsciousness, we can see that they fit into one of these two categories. We are either dealing with our terror of being bad, or we are dealing with our terror of being unimportant and disempowered.

CHAPTER TWENTY FIVE

Conscious Parenting

So what are we to do if we want to move into a more conscious style of parenting?

We must start changing our set of beliefs, replacing the old hurtful ones with new ones that reflect a changing level of consciousness in our parenting.

Here are some indicators of conscious parenting. A conscious parent realizes the following:

1. Parenting is not about teaching, molding, or socializing our children. It is about nurturing them in such a way as to keep the bond between parent and child intact.

2. A conscious parent takes children's thoughts and ideas seriously, genuinely attempting to understand and respect their perspective.

3. Being a conscious parent is to believe that children do want to please their parents and want to remain connected with them at all costs.

4. Being a conscious parent is realizing that every "bad" behavior is a cover up for a bad feeling. Our task as conscious parents is to develop our skill of attunement in order to know what those bad feelings are.

5. Being a conscious parent is knowing that although some behaviors will have to be limited because they are dangerous to either the Self or others, all feelings are acceptable. It is okay to cry, to be afraid, to be shy, to feel sorry for yourself, or to try to get attention.

6. Being a conscious parent is to experience our children as fellow human beings trying to find their way on this planet and to appreciate them for who they are at the moment.

7. Being a conscious parent is to believe that our children are our spiritual equals and that their perspective has equal worth to our own.

8. Being a conscious parent means to voluntarily choose to stop trying to control our children's lives and choose to nurture them instead. Stop making rules and regulations for your children's sake, or as Alice Miller would say, "for their own good."

The thought of getting out of the business of running your children's lives may arouse fears and tension in you. Maybe your fear is that if you don't control their lives, they will control yours. We are often trapped into this dichotomized way of thinking: that one of us has to dominate the other.

9. Being a conscious parent is knowing what your needs are, and learn to set boundaries that are for yourself instead of for your children.

Believe that you have the right as well as the responsibility to set some limits that are for your <u>own good</u>! Once you believe that, you will begin to do it in a warm, caring, and compassionate way that is non-punitive in style. I think that out of our terror that we might be seen as bad or inadequate if our children don't turn out to be "perfect," out of this perceived sense of inadequacy as a human being, out of our deep need to feel powerful, we experience a need to control.

Our need to control is not just a need to control our children, we have a need to control our partners, we have a need to control our colleagues, we have an urge to control everyone! If we have children, our children become a primary target. Because children usually want to please their parents at all costs, and because parents are so powerful in comparison to them, we justify our actions under the guise that we do it for our children's own good. The solution is to do our own personal growth and our own healing work. That's bad news for many parents who come to a parenting workshop or go to a parenting talk in the hope that the speaker is going to tell them how to control their kids! But the more we try to control our children, the more we create a climate of vengeance and rebellion in them.

10. Being a conscious parent means we will be willing to enter into a journey of personal change and personal growth so we lose our need to find redemption in the perfect behavior or the perfect look or the perfect grades of our children. If we begin a journey to learn to feel good about who we are, we will be able to remain grounded in our own goodness and our own innocence and we will be better able to set clear boundaries for ourselves.

11. As conscious parents we will know that such qualities as goodness, kindness, honesty, courage, self confidence, and self discipline are not taught. They are learned by our children experiencing us having those qualities in our interactions with them.

12. As conscious parents we will know that no child becomes loving and kind by being spanked nor by being preached well meaning words. No reprimands, sermons, explanations, threats or prohibitions can make a child capable of love.

A child who is preached at learns to preach. A child who is spanked learns to hit others. A child who is punished by someone bigger than him, learns to take his anger out on someone smaller than him.

Instead, children who are respected, learn respect. Children who are cared for learn to care for those weaker than themselves. Children who are loved for who they are cannot learn intolerance, they learn acceptance. Children raised in a truly loving, supportive environment that is one that conveys, "The you that you are at the moment is acceptable to me even when I have to limit your behavior," will grow up to be our dream children— loving, kind, generous, honest, cooperative, and self confident. They will tap into their life force because they grew up in an environment of loving, generous, and honest kindness.

If you have met with your PIP Group and followed the steps outlined in this book, you are well on your way to becoming a conscious parent.

I want to congratulate you and assure you that you will reap the benefits of your hard work many times over when you and your children experience the fun, the understanding, the closeness, and the deep pleasure that comes from relating to each other with respect and compassion.

CHAPTER TWENTY SIX

Limit Setting – Rewards - Punishments

Why have I put this chapter at the end of the book? Because it takes a greater level of consciousness to comprehend this chapter. It is totally counter to everything you have learned in our culture. Now that you have read this book, it may make more sense to you.

A comment parents often make and which used to puzzle me is, "So you don't believe in setting limits?"

I do believe in setting limits! Setting limits is essential to good parenting. Let me say it another way: There can be no conscious parenting without limit setting. No child can grow up and become a healthy adult if he/she has not encountered limits. But I do suggest a different manner of going about it. Namely, in the problem-solving phase of the Family Round Table, any proposal that is not acceptable to you, you cross out. That is setting a limit. For example your eight-year-old wants to go to bed at 11 pm. While you do write this down (his suggestion), you also write down your desire that he goes to bed by 8 pm. When you evaluate all the possible solutions, you cross out your son's suggestion of going to bed by 11 pm. Clean and direct. No teachy/preachy. No explanations. Just the words, "That one won't work for me." Of course, your son can do the same thing with going to bed by 8 pm. Back to the drawing board until you reach a compromise you can both live with and try for a week.

That sets limits in a manner that is plain and simple. No yelling, no screaming, no shaming, no intimidation, no attempt to control through fear, bullying or guilt. Doing it that way requires personal maturity. It requires that you come to the solution phase with an open mind yet with clarity about your absolute bottom line. It requires that you stand firm on your ground yet remain kind and respectful and that you stay nurturing and compassionate. "You were really hoping that you could go to bed by 11 pm. I bet that would make you feel so grown up. I'm willing to shift it to 8:30 for now with lights out by 9 pm." Try that for a week and evaluate that solution at next week's meeting.

So why do so many parents think that I don't believe in limit setting? I have come to the conclusion that it is because I don't believe in punishment. Apparently in our culture we have come to equate limit setting with punishment. In many people's minds, no punishment means no limits. You let the children run wild.

I do not believe in punishment, AND I do not believe in letting children run wild and out of control.

I do believe that having clarity with regard to what is acceptable to us and what is not and conveying it clearly without blame or judgement is the hallmark of good parenting.

I do not believe in using punishment as a technique to let the children know what we are willing to tolerate and what we are not. I believe in bringing them in and consulting with them so we reach a solution that is mutually acceptable.

A word about rewards and punishments: Natural rewards and punishments are the consequences of life that powerfully influence us. We walk carefully over gravel in our bare feet in order not to be punished by the sharp stones. We love to dive into a cool pool of water when the weather is hot to be rewarded by the refreshment. We don't feel "misunderstood" by nature. Nature shapes our behavior through the use of rewards and punishments. Using rewards and punishments are also powerful ways to train animals. Animals don't think through whether they are being related to fairly or not. But when parents or teachers contrive rewards and punishments, children always feel misunderstood and treated unfairly. Rewards such as gold stars, points, and money have been proven in scientific research to lessen motivation. While punishments such as groundings, time outs, and spankings suppress some behaviors in the short run, they are detrimental to the mental health of children because there develops fear, anger, rebellion, and low self-esteem in the long run. Research shows that the use of rewards proves to be as bad as the use of punishments. In recent years, advisors have urged us to use time out instead of spanking. Certainly this is an improvement over hitting, but the long-term consequences are just as detrimental.

Punishment leads to an inner rebellion. A person who is being punished usually feels misunderstood and treated unfairly. I agree with that perception. If, instead, we are willing to inquire genuinely and really understand, we will discover there is no need to punish. We must talk it through again and again. "Is there anything I (we) can do to be helpful?" "How can we negotiate a middle of the road solution?" "What got in the way?" "Help me understand." Our whole attitude is one that conveys our desire to understand deep in our hearts what it's like to be the child.

Punishment assumes guilt. It implies that there has been wrong doing. It leads to children becoming afraid, afraid of being punished, of course. Enough punishment will lead to anger and rebellion. It will foster a lack of self-confidence and will eventually teach the child, "I am bad." All "bad" behaviors are rooted in the belief that "I am bad."

This is graphically what it looks like. It starts with the belief that the child is bad and therefore deserves punishment.

PUNISHMENT

⬇

FEAR

⬇

ANGER

⬇

REBELLION

⬇

LACK OF SELF CONFIDENCE

⬇

"I AM BAD"

It is when we believe that we are bad that we believe we deserve the punishment. It puts your child on the slippery road of low self-esteem. When we believe we are bad, we behave badly. When we believe we do not deserve to be loved, we behave badly.

On the other hand, limit setting comes from the unshakable belief that you, my dear child are good. So, when you behave in a manner I don't like, something is going on which I may not fully understand (yet). But as I listen to you, I will begin to understand why you behaved the way you did. And it is never because you are bad. It may be that you didn't know, that you are curious, it may be that you needed guidance, or gentle reminders. After all, children have less self-control than adults . . . and how many times have we, the adults, shown poor self control ourselves! The "bad" behavior could be the result of our own unrealistic expectations, our not paying enough attention to our children, our nervousness, our shaming and humiliating them.

When we choose limit setting rather than punishment, we assume the goodness of the child and work together cooperatively to design a workable solution. This increases the children's motivation and helps them want to please us even more. It will foster a good self-image. Since we see and believe in the good in them, despite possible mistakes, they will know that they are valued.

The progression then looks like this. It begins with the assumption that the child is good and needs understanding.

LIMIT SETTING

⬇

COOPERATION

⬇

MOTIVATION

⬇

DESIRE TO PLEASE

⬇

GOOD SELF-IMAGE

⬇

"I AM VALUED"
("They see the good in me.")

Faith in our children means that we believe that at any single moment they are doing their best – just as we are.

162

In a recent Time Magazine lead article on parenting, "Who's In Charge Here?" (August 6, 2001), the author asks, "Can you treat them with respect without sacrificing your authority?. . . Set them free - but still set limits?"

My answer to that is that not only we can, but we must! It is imperative that we learn that setting limits and guiding our children does not have to be harsh, cold, and scary. It is our inner strength that we must develop. If we feel internally well grounded, our limits can be stated in a manner that is gentle and understanding. We do not have to be punitive or humiliating. We need to develop inner strength and inner clarity with our own values. And we need to commit and recommit ourselves to eliminate blame, shame, guilt and any shade of coercion or criticism. For then our children will truly move into their true selves, which is already magnificent.

Here is a comparison of the two styles of discipline:

DISCIPLINE

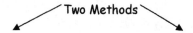
Two Methods

PUNISHMENT
(Time outs, groundings, rewards)

LIMIT SETTING
THROUGH
COOPERATION

- Yes, behavior changes, but out of fear.
- Only situation specific
- Does not internalize
- Does not generalize
- Leads to inhibition and anxiety
- Increased vulnerability to alcohol and drug abuse, and delinquent behavior.
- Physical punishment is not respectful and undermines a child's self-image.
- Leads to stored up anger
- Teaches the child that violence is the way to handle frustrations and anger.

- Behavior changes out of good will and consensus.

- Motivation to change behavior from the inside comes from their relationship with us.

- The child feels understood.

- The connection remains intact.

- Morality develops from trying to be like an admired adult and from feeling good about oneself.

- **Teaches:**

  ### "I AM BAD"

  "My parents don't believe in my goodness."

- **Teaches:**

  ### "I AM VALUED"

  "My parents believe in my goodness."

THE ICEBERG

Next time you feel triggered by your child's behavior, I suggest you say to yourself: "Something's going on and I am feeling triggered." Physically go through the process of taking in a deep breath and hold it for five seconds. This will drain some of your energy and hopefully diffuse your desire to scream at the child or throw out hurtful words, words which you may regret, but can never take back. Then continue your self-talk. "Something's going on, and I may not know what it's about yet, but what I do know is that behavior is only the tip of the iceberg."

The presenting problem is always just that: It's what's visible, it's what catches our attention and we, the parents or the adults are tempted to respond to that "tip of the iceberg behavior" because we do not understand that what is really going on lies below the surface.

Bad behaviors are always an indication that the child is feeling bad. The child needs empathy and understanding from the adults that deeply care for him/her.

Focusing on the behavior, rather than the bad feelings, always makes things worse. It tells the children that we don't understand where they're coming from, that we have no clue into what they are experiencing. The child feels misunderstood and alienated.

It looks like this:

The Iceberg

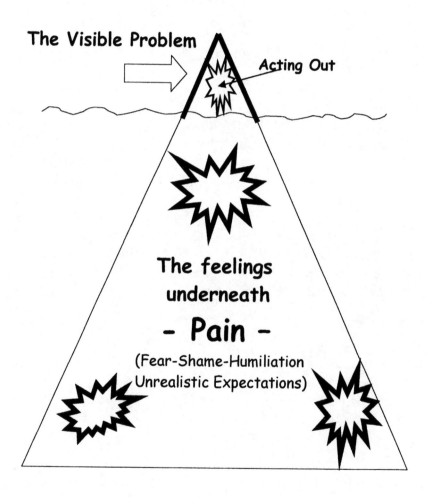

The Visible Problem

Acting Out

The feelings
underneath

- Pain -

(Fear-Shame-Humiliation
Unrealistic Expectations)

Usually, the feeling underneath is pain and the most common pain triggers are:

- Misunderstanding of what the child is trying to accomplish

- Unrealistic expectations (given the child's age and individual skills

- Fear - especially of punishment, of being shamed and of feeling humiliated

These are therefore the questions you want to ask yourself. Are my expectations unrealistic for this particular child? Do I shame and humiliate my child? Am I instilling fear, through rewards (gold stars or happy faces) or punishments (timeouts or groundings)?

Melting the iceberg is a two-step process. You must first start with the bad feelings, acknowledge what's going on underneath and show an empathic understanding, making sure the connection is intact. Only after that, do you take the 2nd step, that of setting limits.

It looks like this:

Melting the iceberg is done from the bottom up

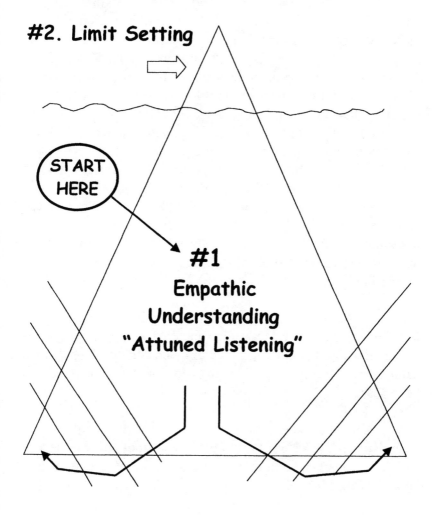

#2. Limit Setting

START
HERE

#1
Empathic
Understanding
"Attuned Listening"

Now go back to Chapter 9 and make sure you set up a weekly time for "The Family Round Table." These concepts along with the Family Round Table will revolutionize your family.

As you have discovered by now, this is a revolutionary book. Children are the last of the abused and oppressed groups in the world. The whole history of the world is a history of groups of people trying to be heard, trying to be valued, and trying to be equal. There has been the movement of slaves becoming free. There has been the movement of blacks gaining a voice in our society. There has been a movement of students getting a say in their education. There has been a movement of gay pride. And the list goes on and on. The over arching movement of them all has been the women's movement. Every group has women and in each movement there is the additional dynamic of women gaining their voice and power. Now in this new century, comes the movement of children gaining their voice. They are equal to adults in their humanness, in their spirituality, in their worth. They must be listened to rather than spoken to. This is our culture's next big journey.

And if we can grasp the enormity of the meanings of this last chapter in all our relationships, maybe we can find peace in this world. Because behind every rock thrower, behind every up rising, behind every enemy, are bad feelings, lots of them, that have never been heard.

And let us never confuse listening with limit setting. We must listen, AND we must set limits. This is not only our new learning as parents, but it is the world's new learning and the only hope for world peace.

Suggested Readings

I have made this handbook purposefully brief and in a light format to reach a larger audience. But should you be someone who likes to read, then here is a suggested reading list. I have only included those books I whole-heartedly recommend! I have listed them alphabetically by title.

Between Parent And Child

Between Parent And Teenager

Teacher And Child

by Haim Ginott, M.D.

You will want to have these books in your child rearing library. These are very practical publications with many clearly written examples and full length dialogues. Helpful in giving you more ideas on how to speak to your children. Could be very useful for additional practice in your PIP Group.

Children The Challenge

by Rudolf Dreckurs, M.D. (with Vicki Sotz, R.N.)

The strength of this book is that it will help you learn how to draw boundaries as a parent. Many parents have trouble setting limits and/or abiding by those they have set. This book is wonderful for that. The weakness is that it does not emphasize the importance of the warm, empathic connection needed with your children.

Child   (a magazine for parents)

Although I sometimes disagree with the psychological perspective given, especially the use of behavioral techniques, still, this magazine is filled with good, practical advice with regards to many parental concerns. It is well worth subscribing to.

Giving The Love That Heals: A guide for parents

by Harville Hendrix and Helen Hunt

This book will be a wonderful companion on your parenting journey. It gives you an in depth look at the developmental stages children go through and how to support them. It will also help you become aware of why "your buttons are pushed" when they are. Where you get stuck with your child is a key to understanding where you got stuck in your own development. Share what you learn about yourself with your PIP Group to take full advantage of this great book. It is a must for every parents library!

How To Talk So Kids Will Listen And Listen So Kids Will Talk

How To Talk So Kids Can Learn At Home And In School

by Adele Faber and Elaine Mazlish

Eminently practical - clear - lots of good illustrations. A wonderful way to get more exposure to very solid principles of parenting. Go, buy, and read their books. All of them!

I'll Never Do To My Kids What My Parents Did To Me

by Thomas Paris, Ph.D. and Eileen Paris, Ph.D.

A guide to conscious parenting. A wonderful book to help you understand the importance of the bond with your children and what to say and do to preserve and strengthen it.

Liberated Parents Liberated Children - Your Guide To A Happier Family

by Adele Faber and Elaine Mazlish

Easy, clear reading on positive, respectful parenting that will build your children's confidence and self esteem.

Magical Child

by Joseph Chilton Pearce

This book is profound and far reaching. Though originally written in the 70's. I just came across it recently and am thoroughly taken by it. It is still in print and enormously educational about the genius of the child's brain and the stages of development it goes through. Pearce does a wonderful job of recommending how parents can work in harmony with nature rather than against it. I strongly recommend it.

Mothering   (a magazine for parents)

This is the best magazine for parents that I have come across. I strongly suggest that you subscribe to it. It is full of valuable information and tools in a context of honoring and respecting both parents and children. A wonderful publication!

Mothering, P.O.Box 1690, Santa Fe, NM 87504-9774

Siblings Without Rivalry

by Adele Faber and Elaine Mazlish

The title tells it all. This is written in the same easy, practical style as in their other books. This will provide you with effective strategies to foster cooperation between your children. A must!

Time Out For Parents - A Compassionate Approach To Parenting

by Cheri Huber and Melinda Guyol, MFCC

A lovely, small, easy reading book for parents who feel stressed; teaching them to slow down and nurture their needs so they, in time, can be emotionally available to their children.

Whole Child Whole Parent

by Polly Berrien Berends

This is a serious book on the meaning of personhood. It is a book of wisdom for those of us who want to use parenthood as a path to spiritual growth.

It is a bit philosophical so may not be for everyone. But if the world of ideas and spirituality intrigues you, this book is for you. In addition, it offers many practical ideas. A true classic!

Your Child's Self-Esteem

by Dorothy Corkille Briggs

An excellent guide to understand what self esteem is and what to do to develop it in your children. A gold mine of practicality and usefulness.

Brief bio of Francine Beauvoir

Francine C. Beauvoir, Ph.D., is a licensed psychologist who received her Ph.D. from the University of Southern California (USC). She was born and raised in France, has been married for over thirty years to psychologist, Bruce Crapuchettes, Ph.D., and has four adult children. She specializes in working with people in relationship - parents, couples and singles. She has trained extensively under Dr. Harville Hendrix in New York and is certified by The Institute For Imago Relationship Therapy in Florida (1-800-729-1121) as an Imago Therapist and a Workshop Presenter. She is also on the faculty there as a Clinical Instructor for Imago Therapy. She is an experienced educator and trains parents, couples and therapists. She is a member of the American Psychological Association and the Association for Imago Relationship Therapy.

Francine is in demand as a speaker and a workshop presenter internationally. She is co-founder of the Pasadena Institute For Relationships, the west coast training center for Imago Relationship Therapy in the United States, and is in private practice.

<u>One-day parenting workshop</u>

Every two or three months, Dr. Beauvoir puts on a parenting workshop. It is very experiential and is presented with a manual that is different from this book.

This book is also available on a two tape audio set.

For more information about the parenting workshop, the audio tapes or this book contact:

Francine C. Beauvoir, Ph.D.

Pasadena Institute For Relationships

2388 N. Altadena Drive
Altadena, California 91001
Ph: 626-798-5242 / Fx: 626-798-2625
www.PasadenaInstitute.com

Also, let me know how you are doing on your parenting journey.
I'd love to hear from you!

- *Francine*